Edwin Abbott Abbott, Edward Rupert Humphreys

Latin Prose through English Idiom

Rules and Exercises on Latin Prose Composition

Edwin Abbott Abbott, Edward Rupert Humphreys

Latin Prose through English Idiom
Rules and Exercises on Latin Prose Composition

ISBN/EAN: 9783337210533

Printed in Europe, USA, Canada, Australia, Japan

Cover: Foto ©Thomas Meinert / pixelio.de

More available books at **www.hansebooks.com**

LATIN PROSE

THROUGH ENGLISH IDIOM.

Rules and Exercises

ON

LATIN PROSE COMPOSITION.

BY THE

REV. EDWIN A. ABBOTT, D.D.,

HEAD MASTER OF THE CITY OF LONDON SCHOOL.

WITH ADDITIONS BY

E. R. HUMPHREYS, A.M., LL.D.,

"LYRA HELLENICA," "MANUALS OF ADVANCED GREEK ETC., &C.

PREFATORY NOTE

BY THE AMERICAN EDITOR.

———◆———

IN using this excellent little Manual with my own pupils, I have felt the want of a series of simpler introductory exercises, illustrative of the "Rules and Reasons," and more especially of those applying to the prepositions; and I have therefore prepared the additional exercises now inserted. I would suggest to teachers the advantage of carrying out the same plan to a much fuller extent while using this text-book.

Much of the difficulty experienced by teachers in communicating, and by pupils in acquiring, a facility in Latin and Greek Composition would be removed, if the former would discard both the idea and the expression so constantly applied to the Greek and Roman tongues, — "the dead languages." Regard them, as what they are, and ever will be, so long as our English tongue survives, "living," and embodying the life-essence of all the best modern tongues, — teach them on the same common-sense, practical plans as you teach German, French, or Spanish, and the duty will become an easier one to the teacher, a pleasanter and more profitable one to the taught.

From the long and successful experience I have had in teaching Latin and Greek composition, it will not, I trust, be deemed presumptuous in me to recommend — as I did, several years ago, in the Introduction to my Livy — as one of the most valuable aids to acquiring correctness and ease of composition, the frequent and close analysis and written translation of passages of Cæsar, Cicero, and Livy, in Latin, and of Xenophon and Plato, in Greek, and then the requiring the pupil on the following day to turn back the translation thus made into Latin or Greek, not insisting on a word-for-word agreement with the original, but allowing new turnings to stand, if not wrong. This last plan I have ever found most encouraging to the pupil.

While the "Scheme of Latin Pronunciation" is retained at the end of the volume, I feel it necessary to say that, beyond the Continental pronunciation of the vowels, which I have advocated and used for nearly twenty years, I dissent in *theory* — as do many scholars far more eminent than I — from many points in that "Scheme," and in the Syllabus, on which it is founded, — a syllabus which, to use the words of one of the professors who prepared it, "has fallen still-born in England." In *practice*, as a tutor for Harvard, I am almost of necessity led into its adoption, having to read with pupils who have been prepared on that system. I earnestly cherish the hope, however, that the Professors of Harvard, and other American Colleges, will yet reconsider this matter of Latin Pronunciation, and modify the rules laid down for the sounds of the consonants.

E. R. H.

293 COLUMBUS AVENUE, Boston,
    July 18, 1876.

PREFACE TO FIRST EDITION.

THE title of this book, "*Latin Prose through English Idiom,*" is not intended to be a meaningless antithesis. The Author's object is to prepare English students for the study and composition of Latin Prose, by calling their attention first to the peculiarities of English idiom, and then to the methods of representing the English in the corresponding Latin idiom.

The first part consists of 'Rules and Reasons.' The pupil is supposed to have gone through a course of Latin Grammar and Latin Exercises, and to be on the point of writing continuous Latin Prose; and this part is intended to give a rapid summary of the Rules of Latin Syntax *regarded from an English point of view.* The differences between English and Latin are not only brought prominently forward, but also, as far as possible, explained. The pupil's attention is called to the points in which English is superior to Latin, to the use of *a* and *the*, to the abundance of Tenses, of Verbal Nouns, and of Compound Prepositions, and, on the other hand, to the Latin superiority in Moods. Rules are not despised, and are frequently and prominently set forth; but an attempt is made to prepare the pupil for them by analysing the English language, and by explaining the force of many English words that were, until lately, seldom explained, e.g. *that, than, of.*

A good deal of space has been given to the Prepositions. It is hoped that the Dictionary of Prepositions contained in Paragraph 41 may be found useful, not only in preventing a good many common blunders made by beginners in Latin Prose, but also in training pupils habitually to connect and explain the different meanings of Prepositions both English and Latin. This seems a very useful mental training.

The Rules are condensed, collected, and numbered at the beginning of the book, for easy reference.

One inconvenience arising from treating the subject generally from an English, but occasionally from a Latin, point of view, is this, that it is difficult to preserve any strictly logical order in the arrangement of the Rules. This would be a very serious defect in a book intended to serve the purpose of a Grammar; but in a book of reference it may, I hope, be excused, provided that the Index at the beginning is found sufficient to guide any moderately careless boy to the explanation and examples of each Rule.

The Examples at the end are purposely unarranged, or rather are arranged with no other object than that, by the time the pupil may be supposed to have forgotten a rule exemplified some six examples back, another exemplification may present itself to him when he is off his guard. Connected examples are very useful to illustrate, but very useless to test a pupil's knowledge. A pupil that knows he is "doing *ut*" may answer correctly enough; but set the same boy on *ut* next day, when he is "doing *quum*," and his correctness will often be lamentably diminished.

In order to serve as a better test, these Examples have not, as the Examples in the former part of the book have, the English peculiarities pointed out by small capitals. The pupil, covering the Latin with his hand, is intended to read off the English into Latin without any help or guidance whatever.

The Exercises are arranged on a principle that I have adopted for many years, and that I may call *the pitfall principle*. Each Exercise contains a number of pits or traps. All traps that prove fatal are repeated in the following Exercise, in a disguised form. If the fatality continues, the traps are repeated, always masked in different expressions, until even the weakest pupil in the class gains experience enough to warn him of danger. An instance will explain what is meant. In the first exercise of the term, the teacher sets, perhaps, "The excellent Balbus answered in haste, 'I asked you to come to Rome, and you promised to do so,' &c." The bottom boy sends up, "Egregius Balbus respondit celeritate, rogavi te venire ad Romam et tu promisisti facere ita." The teacher points out the correct expression in each case:—(1) "Balbus, vir egregius"; (2) "summa celeritate," or "celeriter"; (3) "'rogavi' inquit"; (4) "ut venires"; (5) "Romam," without "ad"; (6) "te id facturum esse." Then he sets something like the following (only carefully dispersing the different traps through different parts of the new exercise):—"'I am surprised,' said (3) the passionate (1) queen, 'that, though I repeatedly entreated you (4) to come with (2) speed to my assistance, you have made a foolish promise to remain at (5) Carthage.'" Here our five old pitfalls are re-introduced, and one or two, not worth now mentioning, are introduced for the first time. It is needless to say that the bottom boy will fall into the same pitfall four or five, or even, on the subject of Sequence of Tenses and Oratio Obliqua, ten times; but at last even the dullest avoid some pitfalls, and are found to have been goaded or wearied into something approximating to thought.

The Exercises are selected out of some hundreds dictated in the course of an experience of several years. The English will occasionally be found abrupt, disconnected, and, it need not be said, uninteresting. I hope, however, that the language will be found free from the worst fault of such exercises—the fault of blending English and Latin into a Latin-English mixture that is no language at all, and that serves to teach nothing. The Exercises are meant rather as specimens of the kind of teaching than as models. Each teacher will do well to dictate, or, still better (if he has time), to write, exercises of his own. But though apologies may be due for the execution, I believe the *pitfall principle* to be extremely useful and stimulating, and I think the practice of writing continuous Latin Prose in this way might be advantageously taught much earlier than it is taught at present. Boys are wearied to death by years of "Exercises on Rules"; and the monotony of the exercise tends to suppress thought.

Some of the Exercises consist of extracts from the *Percy Anecdotes*, modified for the purpose of exemplifying the differences between Latin and English idiom. In almost all of them will be found constantly recurring exemplifications of the more important rules of Latin Prose, *e.g.* the *Sequence of Tenses*, the use o 'ut' for *to*, and, above all, the rules of *Oratio Obliqua*. To this last I attach great importance, for I am persuaded that a boy cannot be taught to master *Oratio Obliqua* without having been at the same time taught, in some degree, to think.

Although I fear that many pupils even in Sixth Forms might consult parts of this little book with advantage, yet it is not intended for them, and hardly touches on style. It does not, therefore, cover the same ground as Mr. Potts' "*Hints towards Latin Prose Composition*," from which many of my pupils have gained great help.

The 'Scheme of Latin Pronunciation,' at the end of the book, is based on the Syllabus recently issued by the Latin Professors of Cambridge and Oxford, at the repeated request of the Head Masters of Schools.

PREFACE TO SECOND EDITION.

THE Alphabetical Index, the changes in the headings of the pages, the easier introductory exercises, and the Appendix on the connection of sentences, introduced into this Edition, will, it is hoped, materially increase the utility of the book.

The knowledge that the First Edition had been prepared somewhat hurriedly for the press prevented me from acknowledging the kind help of several friends, whose names I was unwilling to connect with a possible responsibility for mistakes for which I alone was responsible. In issuing this corrected and revised Edition I feel bound to express my especial obligations to Mr. J. S. Phillpotts, one of the Assistant Masters of Rugby, for his general supervision of the work from the first, and in particular for the Appendix in this edition, which is abridged from a sketch drawn out by him; also to the Rev. J. H. Lupton, Sur-Master of St. Paul's School, and to Mr. Henry Lee-Warner, one of the Assistant Masters of Rugby, for several valuable suggestions and corrections. My acknowledgments would be incomplete without reference to the help given me, in the course of preparing this Edition, by Mr. H. J. Roby—help that increases my regret that the second volume of his Latin Grammar is still a hope deferred.

CONTENTS.

	PAGE
RULES *	xiii
RULES AND REASONS	1—106
MISCELLANEOUS IDIOMS	107—130
GRADUATED EXERCISES	131—161
SCHEME OF LATIN GENDERS	162
SCHEME OF LATIN PRONUNCIATION	163
APPENDIX ON THE CONNECTION OF SENTENCES .	164
ALPHABETICAL INDEX	166

* These Rules will be found to serve the purpose of a detailed Index to pages 1—106.

INDEX OF RULES.

These Rules are intended to be committed to memory, and are therefore expressed as tersely as possible, without attempt at illustration. For explanations and examples, the pupil is referred, by the figures in brackets, to the Paragraphs in the 'Rules and Reasons.' For instance Rule 92 simply states the Latin use of Verbs of fearing. For the explanation, the pupil is referred to Paragraph 49.

The Index will also serve as a detailed Table of Contents to the 'Rules and Reasons.'

1. THERE is a reason for every irregularity. (1)

2. Latin-derived words in English can seldom be represented by their Latin originals. (2)

3. Many English words, especially abstract Nouns, have no single corresponding words in Latin. (3, 3 *a*)

4. The English Passive should often be rendered by the Latin Active. (4)

5. Do not translate the redundant *it* nor *that* in '*that* of.' (5)

6. '*It is the duty,*' '*must,*' &c. are often rendered by the Latin Neuter Gerundive with Dative of the Person. (5)

7. I have a book = est **mihi** liber. (5)

8. Latin Verbs taking the Dative in the Active must be used impersonally in the Passive, retaining the Dative, *e.g.* 'tibi a me **indulgetur.**' (6)

9. **Quisquam** and **ullus** are used in Negative and Comparative Sentences, and in Interrogative Sentences that expect the answer 'no.' (7)

10. *Each* returned to his tent = Ad **suum quisque** tabernaculum **rediere.** (7)

11. Distinguish **alter** and **alius, quis** and **uter.** (7)

12. Observe the different meanings of '*one.*' (8)

13. Avoid Pronouns and the repetition of Nouns, as far as possible, by using the same Subject or Object for different sentences. (9)

14. **Nostrum** and **vestrum** are used partitively; **nostri** and **vestri** in other cases. (10)

14.* **Se,** not **is** nor **ille,** refers to the principal Subject. (10 *a*)

15. Use **nullius, nullo,** for **neminis, nemine.** (10)

16. The English Passive Indicative Present, *e.g.* 'is caught, is ambiguous, and must be translated, according to the sense, by the Latin Present or Perfect. (11)

17. The English Imperfect after *while* is often rendered by the Latin Present. (11)

18. The English Pluperfect after *till, before,* and *after* is often rendered by the Latin Perfect. (11)

19. The English Present after *when, if, as long as, unless, before,* and *after,* is often to be rendered by the Latin Future. (11)

20. Be careful in the use of the English Auxiliary Verbs. Remember that they are used Subjunctively as well as Indicatively, and that they often have their original, as well as their Auxiliary, force. (12)

21. 'I ought to, could, *have done*,' is, in Latin, 'debui, potui, **facere**.' (12)

22. Do not fear = ne **timueris**; not, ne **timeas**. (12)

23. Verbs of *trusting, pleasing, helping, hurting, yielding to, suiting, resisting, favouring, envying, being angry with*, take the Dative. (13)

24. I threaten you with death = minor **tibi mortem**.

25. Adjectives similar in meaning to the Verbs in Rule 23, and also Adjectives expressing likeness or unlikeness and proximity, take the Dative. (13)

26. Verbs of *fulness, want*, &c. take the Ablative. (13)

27. **Pudet, pœnitet, piget, miseret, tædet** take the Accusative of the Person feeling, and the Genitive of that which causes the feeling. (13*a*)

28. Write 'interest **Tullî**' but 'interest **mea, tua, nostra**, &c.' (13*a*)

29. **Misereor, obliviscor**, and **reminiscor** take the Genitive. (13*a*)

30. **Fungor, fruor, utor, vescor, pascor**, and **potior** take the Ablative. (13*a*)

31. **Doceo, celo, rogo, oro**, and **interrogo** take two Accusatives. (14)

32. So do **moneo, admoneo**, and **hortor**, when the Accusative of the thing is a neuter Pronoun. (14)

33. **Transduco** and **transporto** take two Accusatives. (14)

34 Verbs compounded of Prepositions, and implying motion, take the Dative of the Indirect Object, if they are used metaphorically, *e.g.* 'princeps **imperatori milites** detraxit.' (15)

35. If literally used, they require the repetition of the Preposition, *e.g.* 'anulum **de digito** detraxit.' (15)

36. He flung himself at Cæsar's feet = **Cæsari** se ad pedes projecit. (15)

37. Verbs signifying *preferring* and the *contrary* take the Dative of the Indirect Object. (15)

38. After a verb of *motion to*, names of towns and small islands are in the Accusative without a Preposition. So are **domum, humum,** and **rus.** (16)

39. After a verb of *motion from*, the above-mentioned words are in the Ablative without a Preposition. (16)

40. After a verb of *rest in*, the above-mentioned words are, if Singular, in a locative case ending in -i (but **Roma-i** is written **Romæ**): if Plural, in the Ablative. (16)

41. **Sum, do, duco, tribuo** take a double Dative, *e.g.* 'librum **mihi dono** dedit.' (17)

42. *The* brave Balbus = Balbus, vir fortissimus. (18)

43. Two or more Adjectives are not attached to the same Noun without **et** or **que.** (19)

44. *This disgraceful* calamity = **hæc tam fœda** calamitas. (19)

45. *The* men in the ship = **qui erant in navi.** (20)

46. *The* sooner, *the* better = **quo** citius, **eo** melius. (21)

47. Distinguish between *a* meaning *any*, and *a* meaning *a certain*. (22)

48. No poet = **nemo** poeta. (22)

49. *Every one* of *superior* learning } = { doctissimus
    All the most learned men } = { quisque. (22)

50. **Omnis** means *all* and not *every*, in Prose. (22)

51. (a) 1,000 *or* } = { (a) **mille milites.**
    (b) 10,000 men }   { (b) decem **millia militum.**

52. More learning = **plus doctrinæ.**

53. Participles are freely used as Adjectives in English, but not in Latin, *e.g.* 'the *despairing* soldiers,' 'milites, **jam desperantes,**' but not '**desperantes milites.**' (23)

54. *With* and *in*, denoting *manner*, must not be translated by the *simple Ablative of a Noun unqualified by an Adjective*, e.g. '*in* anger,' '*with* fury' = **iracunde,** or N.B. **summa** iracundia. (24)

55. **Nunc** refers to the Present, simply; **jam** to the Present regarded with reference to the Past or Future. (25)

56. *More*, when used with Verbs and meaning *to a greater extent*, is **plus**: when used with Adjectives, and when meaning *rather*, it is **magis.** (26)

57. Extension of time or space is expressed by the Accusative. (27)

58. The Ablative denotes the time *at which* or *within which* anything is completed. (28)

59. Definite price is expressed by the Ablative. (29)

60. **Tanti, quanti, pluris, minoris** (but on the other hand, **magno, parvo, plurimo, &c.**) are used after Verbs of *selling* and *buying*. (29)

61. **Tanti, quanti, pluris, minoris,** with **magni, parvi, plurimi** and **minimi,** and also **nihili,** are used *after verbs of estimation*, and after **est,** signifying *it is worth*. (29)

62. Adjectives, as well as Verbs, denoting fulness and emptiness, are followed by the Genitive or Ablative. (30, 31)

63. Some Participles that are used as Adjectives take an Ablative of the quasi-Instrument, *e.g.* 'contentus **parvo.**' (32)

64. **Dignus** and **indignus** take the Ablative. (32)

65. **Natus, satus,** and **ortus** take the Ablative. (32)

66. An English Preposition between two Nouns, if it denotes that the second is the Object of the first, is often expressed by the Latin Genitive, as '**militiæ** vacatio,' 'exemption from service.' (33)

67. Present Participles used as quasi-Nouns, and some Adjectives in -**ax**, take the Genitive, *e.g.* 'patiens **laboris**,' '**capax imperii.**' (34)

68. An English Preposition denoting that a Noun is the Object of an Adjective is often rendered by the Genitive, as '**perfidiæ** imperitus.' (35)

69. Verbs of *condemning*, as well as of *accusing* and *acquitting*, take the Genitive of the charge. (36)

70. *Of* preceding a Noun denoting a *quality* is rendered by combining an Adjective and Noun in the Genitive or Ablative. (37)

71. It is *the mark of, characteristic of, like,* &c. are often expressed by the Genitive. (38)

72. English Prepositions denoting *rest* must often be rendered by Latin Prepositions denoting *motion*, e.g. 'on our journey,' '**ex** itinere.' (39)

73. Do not translate redundant *of*, e.g. 'the City *of* London.' (40)

74. *Of* is often rendered in Latin by combining an Adjective or Participle with a Noun, *e.g.* 'summus mons,' 'the top of the mountain.' (40)

The English Prepositions in Alphabetical order are arranged, with their Latin equivalents, on pages 31—57. (41)

75. *By*, denoting *agency*, requires **a** or **ab** before the Ablative. Page 57.

76. *In* when expressing *direction* literally or metaphorically, is followed by the Accusative. Page 44.

77. **Cum** is an enclitic after **me, te, nobis, vobis, quo, quibus.** Page 56.

78. The measure of excess or defect is expressed by the Ablative, *e.g.* 'quinque **pedibus** major.' (42)

Idioms involving Conjunctions and the Relative Pronoun, are arranged in Paragraphs 43 to 72.

79. Thomas, John, and Henry = Thomas, Johannes, Henricus; or Thomas **et** Johannes **et** Henricus. (44)

80. **Autem, enim, que, quidem, ve** and **vero,** and generally **igitur,** cannot stand first in a sentence. (44*a*)

81. **Sed** corrects or denies: **autem** (δέ) introduces something not inconsistent with what has gone before: **at** introduces a clause abruptly. (44 *a*)

82. 'And not,' 'and no one,' 'and never,' 'if . . . not,' are **neque, nec quisquam, neque unquam, nisi.** (45)

83. I *say* it is *not* true = **Nego** hæc vera esse. (45)

84. Do not say 'ne quidem Balbus,' but 'ne Balbus quidem.' (45)

85. 'And he,' 'now this,' &c. must often be rendered by **qui, quod,** &c. *e.g.* 'now when he heard *this*,' '**quæ** quum audivisset.' (46)

86. 'He also said' = '**idem** dixit.' (46)

87. He burned *and* left the bridge = Pontem **incensum** deseruit. (47)

88. *That* introducing an Objective or Subjective clause is generally to be rendered by the Infinitive. (48)

89. Avoid the ambiguity arising from the Double Accusative before and after an Infinitive, *e.g.* 'Aio **te** Æacida **Romanos** vincere posse.' (48)

90. It seems *that* } he is honest.
There is no doubt *that*
{ Videtur **honestus** esse.
{ Haud dubium est **quin** honestus sit. (49)

91. There is no doubt *that he will be caught* = Haud dubium est **quin futurum sit** ut capiatur. (49)

92. I fear *that* he will come = Vereor (timeo &c.) **ne** veniat. I fear *that* he will not come = Vereor **ut** veniat. (49)

93. I heard her sing = audivi illam **canentem**. (50)

94. *Whether*, introducing a Subjective or Objective clause, is **num** or '**utrum** . . . . **an**': introducing a condition, it is **sive**. (51)

95. Where the Relative introduces *a thought*, and not a mere *fact*, it is followed by the Latin Subjunctive. (52)

96. The Subjunctive generally follows '**sunt qui**,' '**erant qui**,' *i.e.* 'there are, were, some *(such) that*.' (52)

97. **Qui** takes the Subjunctive when introducing a statement made by some one distinct from the writer. (52)

98. *What* in Dependent Interrogatives must be rendered by **quid** and followed by the Subjunctive. (53)

99. When *the* qualifying an Antecedent implies *great* or *many*, **quantus** or **quot** should be used instead of the Relative, *e.g.* 'I perceived *the* kindness with which, &c. 'intellexi **quanta** benevolentia me exciperet.' (53)

100. 'The most beautiful *that*,' 'all *that*,' 'the men *that*,' must not be translated literally in Latin. (54)

100*a*. The Relative in Latin often precedes its Antecedent.

101. There was no one *that* {did not weep / he did not punish} = Nemo erat { **quin** fleret. / **quem non** puniret. (55)

102. There was not one *but* hated him = Nemo erat **quin** illum odisset. (55)

103. The English Antecedent, when in apposition to a preceding sentence, is attracted into the Relative clause in Latin, *e.g.* 'he lightened the taxes, an *act* that endeared him to the people,' '**quo beneficio** gratus in vulgus factus est.' (56)

104. Not a day passes *that* he does *not* come = Dies fere nullus **quin** homo ventitet. (57)

105. Beware of the English omitted Relative with Participles, *e.g.* 'those *remaining* here,' '**qui** hic manent. (58)

106. Who would believe such a man *as*, or, a man *like*, Catiline? = Quis Catilinæ, **homini impurissimo**, credat? (60)

107. When two words are connected in the way of comparison by **quam**, and when the Verb is the same for each member of the sentence of Comparison, the two words stand in the same case, *e.g.* '**Tullius** melior est quam **Balbus**.' (61)

108. **Quam** cannot be replaced by the Ablative of the second member of the comparison unless the first member of the comparison is in the Nominative or Accusative, *e.g.* 'donum dedit specie majus **quam** re,' not 'majus re.' (62)

109. Take care not to use the Ablative instead of **quam**, where the Adjective does not qualify either member of the Comparison, *e.g.* 'he has a taller horse than I' is not

'Ille equum altiorem habet **me**,' but '**quam** ego (habeo).' (63)

110. '*Sequence of Tenses.*' In subordinate sentences, the Tenses depend on the Tenses of the principal sentence, the rule being '*Like follows like*,' e.g. 'Do you know where he *was?*' 'Scisne ubi **fuerit?**' (64)

111. I do not know what I should have done = Nescio quid **facturus fuerim.** (64)

112. **Quum** with the Imperfect and Pluperfect generally takes the Subjunctive. (66)

113. **Postquam** takes the Perfect unless an interval is expressed or emphatically implied. (66)

114. **Antequam** and **priusquam, dum, donec** and **quoad** are followed by the Subjunctive when design is implied, or when an action is referred to that has not actually commenced. (66)

115. *Not because* it is honourable, *but because* it is useful = **Non quod** honestum **sit**, sed **quia** utile **est.** (68)

116. '**Si**' with the Past Tenses of the Subjunctive denotes an impossible, '**si**' with the Present Tenses a possible, condition. (69)

117. You must never have different tenses of the Subjunctive in the Protasis and Apodosis. (69)

118. **Quanquam** generally takes the Indicative, **quamvis** the **Subjunctive.** (69)

119. **Quamvis** is often used with an Adjective, without a Verb. (69)

120. You will repent, *when old* = **Senem** te pœnitebit. (70)

121. He is frivolous, *if not* immoral = Levis est, **no dicam** improbus. (70)

INDEX OF RULES.

122. Instead of **ut non, ut nemo, ut nunquam**, write **ne, ne quis, ne quando**, where purpose is denoted. (72)

123. **Utinam** with the Present Subjunctive introduces wishes that can be realized: with the Past Subjunctive, wishes that cannot. (72)

'*To*,' *different uses of.* (73)

124. '*To*,' denoting *purpose*, must never be expressed by the Latin Infinitive. (73)

125. I *promise, hope, to* come = **promitto, spero**, me **venturum** esse. (73)

126. I hope that it is so = **spero rem ita se habere.** (73)

127. *I happened to* = **accidit ut** (ego) &c. (73)

128. *To*, after Verbs of *asking, commanding, advising*, and *striving* must be rendered by **ut** with the Subjunctive. Exceptions, **jubeo, conor.** (73)

129. The English Present Participle, inasmuch as it often contains a concealed Conjunction, can seldom be rendered by the Latin Present Participle. (74)

130. After **ad** and **in** use the Gerundive and not the Gerund, if the Verb takes an Accusative Object. (75)

131. The Gerund or Gerundive is used after **ad, de, in, inter**, and **ob**, seldom after other Prepositions. (75)

The English Prepositions used with Verbals are arranged in Alphabetical order in pages 93—96. (75)

132. The Subject of the principal Verb often comes earlier in a Latin sentence than in English, so as to dispense with **is** and **ille.** (76)

133. Use Parentheses to avoid Pronouns. (77)

134. In Oratio Recta leave the introductory sentence unfinished, and place **inquit** (not **dixit** or **respondit**) after the first emphatic word of the speech. (78)

135. In passing from Oratio Recta to Oratio Obliqua, (1) principal Verbs fall into the Infinitive Mood and their Subjects into the Accusative; (2) the Tenses of the Indicative are preserved in the Infinitive; (3) where the Future Infinitive does not exist, the form **fore ut** is used; (4) the Subjunctive in the Apodosis* of a Conditional sentence is rendered by the Future Participle with **esse** or **fuisse**. (78 *a*)

136. In passing from Oratio Recta to Oratio Obliqua (5) Indicatives following **si, qui** and Conjunctions derived from **qui**, are changed into Imperfect or Pluperfect Subjunctives; (6) Imperatives become Imperfect Subjunctives; (7) Questions in the Second Person are rendered by the Imperfect Subjunctive; (8) Questions in the First or Third Person, by the Accusative and Infinitive; (9) **me** will become **se, hic** will become **illic**, &c. (78 *b—e*)

137. To diminish the ambiguity arising from the use of *he* in English Oratio Obliqua, use **ipse** in Latin to shew the reference of **se**. (78 *f*)

138. In Oratio Obliqua the introductory sentence is often completed. (78 *g*)

139. Metaphors cannot be literally translated from English into Latin. (79)

140. Hyperbole cannot always be literally translated, *e.g.* I prefer a *thousand* deaths = malo **sexcenties** mori. (80)

---

* For the meaning of this word, see page 81.

LATIN PROSE
THROUGH ENGLISH IDIOM

RULES AND REASONS.

1. Irregularities. When we find an irregularity in Latin or in any other language—'at Corinth,' '**Corinthi**' —we ought to feel sure that there is some reason for it. Sometimes we can find a reason. For example, why is 'at Carthage' '**Carthagini**,'* apparently, dative; and 'at Corinth' '**Corinthi**,' genitive? The explanation is said to be that the -*i* in **Corinthi, Carthagini, Romai** (-æ), **domi** is an old locative case.

Sometimes we cannot find a reason. For example, why do the Latins say '**Nemini** faveo,' but dislike to say '**Neminis** misereor,' preferring '**nullius** misereor'? No explanation, that I know of, has been given of this. But, whether we can find out a reason or not, we must always bear in mind that:

Rule—There is a reason for every irregularity.

2. Latin-derived words. In almost all cases English words derived from Latin do not now mean the

* The form in -e is also found. It has been suggested that the -**i** is used in familiar names, *e.g.* **Carthagini**, but -e in others, *e.g.* **Præneste**.

same as the Latin cognates, e.g. *oppress* must not be rendered by **opprimo**, which means *I crush* or *surprise*.

Rule—Do not* translate English words of Latin derivation by Latin cognates.

Examples : *secure, honest, office, occupy, obtain, observe, censure, person, station, family, inspiration, succeed, conspire, cease, probable, expect.*

3. Complex thoughts. It is natural that the language of a modern civilized nation should contain many more words expressing complex thoughts, than are found in the language of an ancient nation. Periphrases must be used to express such modern words in the ancient language, *e.g.* **res novæ** for *a revolution*, **res adversæ** for *adversity*. Some metaphors, e.g. *striking* in 'a *striking* thought,' cannot be literally translated into Latin. See Paragraph 79.

3a. Abstract Nouns may be rendered, (1) by periphrases, e.g. *theory*, **præcepta artis, quod in præceptis positum est**, (2) by Verbs, *e.g.* 'In pursuit of some cherished *object*, they will undergo any *hardship*, and submit to any *degradation*,' '**quidvis perpetiuntur, cuivis deserviunt,** dum quod velint consequantur.' See Par. 40.

Rule—Many English words represent complex thoughts for which there are no single words in Latin.

4. The emphatic subject. In English, if we wish to emphasize the Subject, e.g. *John* in '*John* built this house,' we have to use redundant *it*, '*It was John that*,' &c., or the Passive '*The house was built by*,' &c. In Latin the Subject can be emphasized by the *order* of the words, and therefore need not be emphasized by *construction*. Hence :—

Rule—The English Passive should often be rendered by the Latin Active. Thus

---

* That is, do not without verification or care.

The soldiers WERE SEIZED *with a panic*	Milites **cepit** pavor

5. The redundant 'it.' To avoid an unemphatic termination, *e.g.* 'That the man committed suicide *is said*,' (and perhaps to indicate the construction early in the sentence) the English insert a redundant *it*. The Latins never use this redundancy.

IT *is said that the man committed suicide*	**Ferunt hominem** } mortem **Homo fertur** } sibi conscivisse

'*That*' is often used for a previous Substantive to avoid repeating it before a Preposition, generally '*of*,' e.g. 'I would rather abide by my judgment than by *that* of all the rest.' It is omitted in Latin. 'Meo judicio stare malo quam ( ) omnium reliquorum.' Sometimes the Substantive is repeated, 'quam **judicio**.' *But never use* **is** *or* **ille** *to represent the English* '*that*' *in* '*that of*.'

Rule—Do not translate the redundant 'it,' nor 'that' in 'that of.'

Sentences stating a duty or necessity, e.g. '*it* is the duty of Balbus to avoid this,' are often turned in Latin as follows: 'The avoiding of this is for Balbus,' 'Balbo hoc vitandum est.' From Intransitive verbs the Neuter of the Gerundive is used impersonally, *e.g.* 'all *must* die,' 'omnibus est moriendum,' *i.e.* 'there is to be dying for all.'

Rule—'It is the duty,' 'must,' &c., are often rendered by the Neuter of the Latin Gerundive with the Dative of the person referred to. So 'I have' = 'est mihi.'

6. The English Passive. If an Active Verb in English takes a Preposition between itself and its Objects, *e.g.* 'I trust to you,' we rarely venture to say in the Passive 'you are trusted to.' If the Preposition is to be kept, we must say 'trust is given to you.' So, in Latin, where Verbs in the Active take the Dative of the Object, you must not place that Object as the Subject of the Passive Verb, but must retain the *Dative* and use the Verb *impersonally*, e.g. '**Tibi creditur,**' 'there is trust given to you.'

N.B.—Such verbs are very few, but some of them are very common : **persuadeo, noceo, credo, placeo, ignosco, faveo.**

Rule—Latin Verbs taking the Dative must be used impersonally in the Passive, retaining the Dative.

7. Pronouns. The English *anyone* is ambiguous. Distinguish between (1) **quisquam*** or **ullus**, (2) **quilibet** or **quivis** (which means *anyone you like*), and (3) **aliquis** (*someone, any particular person*).

| ANYONE *can boast that he is more learned than* ANY *of his own pupils* | **Cuilibet** promptum est gloriari se doctiorem esse quam **quemquam** suorum discipulorum |

Rule—'**Quisquam**' and '**ullus**' are used in negative and comparative sentences, and in interrogative sentences expecting '**no.**'

This is sometimes expressed thus: where *all* are excluded use **ullus** or **quisquam,** where *all* are included use **quivis** or **quilibet.**

The beginner must also distinguish between (1) **alter** *the other (of two)*, and **alius** *another*; (2) **uter ?** *which (of two)?* and **quis** or **qui ?** *which ?* And (3) between **uterque** *each of two*, and **quisque** *each.*

* It ought to be unnecessary to warn the pupil against confounding **quisquam** with **quisque** *each*, and **quisquis** *whoever*. But it may be useful to remind him of the position of **quisque** immediately after **suus,** the Verb being in the *Plural,* in such sentences as 'they returned to their several tents,' 'Ad **suum quisque** tabernaculum **rediere.**'

8. One in the sense of *people, we, a man*, as in '*One* sees every day,' &c., must be translated by **nos, omnes**, &c. or by the Impersonal Passive, *e.g.* '*One* ought not to fear,' 'non est **timendum**.' After *if,* use the Second Person (not inserting **tu**) or **quis**, *e.g.* 'If *one* does one's best,' 'Si **agis** or **quis agit**, pro viribus.'

'*One . . . another*' is '**alius . . . alius**'; '*the one . . . the other*' is '**alter . . . alter**.'

One, unless used as a numeral meaning *one and not more than one*, is never to be translated by **unus**. The neglect of this rule is as faulty as the French-English use of *one:* 'I have *one* book' for 'I have *a* book.'

Rule—Observe the different meanings of 'one.'

9. One, when referring to a preceding Substantive, must be left untranslated in Latin, or must be translated by repeating the Substantive, as in 'a small house is better than a large *one*,' 'quam **magna** (domus).' Here the Adjective with its inflection renders the repetition of the Substantive unnecessary.

Avoid, wherever you can, the repetition of the Substantive represented by *one*. 'I haven't a horse of my own, but my brother lends me *one*,' 'Equum equidem non habeo; frater autem mihi commodat.'

9a. Pronouns are not so often used in Latin as in English. The Latin Participle facilitates the omission of Pronouns, *e.g.* 'I saw my brother yesterday, and gave *him* a book,' 'Fratri, **viso** heri, librum dedi.' The Latins also omit Pronominal Adjectives often where the context leaves little room for ambiguity, *e.g. my* is omitted in the last example, and so, 'Tell *your* brother,' 'Dic fratri.' The Latin use of inflections diminishes the ambiguity arising from such omissions.

Rule—Avoid Pronouns, and the repetition of Nouns, as far as possible, by using the same Subject or Object for the different parts of the same sentence. See Paragraph 76.

10. Pronouns, anomalies in.

The Latins have two words to denote *us* and *you* in the Genitive, one **nostri**, signifying *us* and *you* collectively, the other **nostrum**, *us* and *you* distributively. **Nostri** appears to be the Genitive of the Adjective **noster** used substantively. **Nostri** means 'of our nature,' 'of our interests,' 'of our condition.' **Nostrum** is the true plural, and means simply 'of us,' 'of our number.' Thus, 'none *of us*' is 'nemo **nostrum**' (partitive), but 'our mind is the best part *of us*, i.e. *of our nature*,' is '**nostri** melior pars animus est.' Roughly speaking, we may say:

Rule—' Nostrum,' ' vestrum ' are used partitively; otherwise ' nostri,' ' vestri.'

That this rule is not strictly true is seen from the fact that, when **omnium** precedes the Genitive of **nos** or **vos**, it is necessary (not merely allowable) to have **nostrum** or **vestrum**, even used Possessively. ' Patria est communis **omnium nostrum** * parens.' The reason is that **omnium** brings into prominence the *multitudinous* or *distributive* side of **nos**.

No satisfactory reason has been given, as yet, of:

Rule—' Nullius' and ' nullo' are used instead of ' neminis' and ' nemine.'

10a. Him. In Early English, *him* often refers to the Subject, *e.g.* 'he gat *him* home.' This is sometimes ambiguous, so we now add *self* ('*same*'), *unless another Subject intervenes between ' him' and the Subject to which ' him' refers*, e.g. 'he helped *himself*,' but 'he said that Balbus helped *him*.' The Latins generally (but see 78 f.) use **se** to refer to the principal Subject, whether another Subject intervenes or not; 'Dixit Balbum **sibi** subvenisse.'

Rule—Se (not eum nor illum) refers to the Principal Subject.

11. English Tenses are superior to Latin in their variety. There is nothing in Latin to distinguish between *I catch* and *I am catching*; between *I caught, I have caught*.

* **Nostrum** cannot be Genitive dependent on **omnium**.

and *I have been catching.* Sometimes '*I am catching*' may be rendered '**In eo sum ut capiam**' or '**jam capio.**' '*I have caught ten fish*' may be sometimes rendered '*decem pisces* **captos habeo**;' '*I have been for two days catching fish,*' '*biduum* **jam** *pisces* **capio.**' On the other hand, the English Passive is ambiguous :—

The catcher is CAUGHT	**Captus est** captor
You are LOVED, *I am* HATED	Tu quidem **amaris,** mihi autem **invidetur**

Rule—The ambiguous Eng. Pres. Pass. form, *e.g.* ' are built,' must be rendered, according to the sense, by the Latin Pres. or Perf.

Note the following differences of idiom :

WHILE *this* WAS GOING ON, *the enemy fled*	**Dum** hæc **geruntur,** hostes terga dederunt

Rule—The English Incomplete Past (Imperfect) after *while* is graphically rendered in Latin by the Present after ' dum.'

I did not let him go TILL *he* HAD PROMISED *to refrain from it for the future*	Hominem non **ante** dimisi **quam promisit** se ab his in posterum temperaturum esse
AFTER *the fate of the war* HAD BEEN DECIDED, *he used often to live at Rome*	Postquam victoria constituta **est,** Romæ erat frequens

Rule—The English Complete Past (Pluperfect) when following the Conjunctions ' Till,' ' Before,' and ' After,' is often rendered by the Latin Perfect (Aorist).

When a long interval is expressed or implied, **postquam** is sometimes followed by the Pluperfect. If **quum** is used, see Paragraph 66.

AUXILIARY VERBS.

In saying *if*, or *when* 'he *comes*,' instead of '*shall* or *shall have* come,' we speak idiomatically but incorrectly. The Latin is more correct than the English idiom. *If*, till recent times, was followed by the Subjunctive inflection in English, but this has died out.

He will do it if he IS ABLE	Faciet, si **poterit**
I will set out when day BREAKS	Quum **illucescet**, (better **illuxerit**) proficiscar

In dependent sentences there are other important differences in the use of Tenses: see Paragraph 64.

Rule—The English Present Tense after 'When,' 'If,' 'As long as,' 'Unless,' is often to be rendered by the Latin Future.

12. The Auxiliary Verbs in English require care in rendering them into Latin.

For example, *would* is the past of *will* or *wish*: and 'he *would* do it, in spite of me,' means 'he *wished*' (Indicative). But 'he *would* do it, if you asked him,' means 'he *would wish*' (Subjunctive). So 'he *could*' may mean 'he *was* able,' or 'he *would be* able.' Note the following:—

He MAY (*possibly*) *come*	**Fieri potest ut** veniat
You MAY *come* (*if you like*)	**Licet** tibi venire
He MIGHT *help me if he* WOULD	**Posset** mihi subvenire, modo si **vellet**
He MIGHT *have helped me, but he* WOULD *not*	**Potuit**, sed **noluit**, mihi subvenire
He MIGHT *return at any moment*	**Fieri potest ut** quamvis subito redeat
I WOULD *pardon you if you* WOULD *help yourself* (*which you will not do*)*	Si modo tibi ipse **subvenires**, ego tibi **ignoscerem**

* For rules about the Tenses of the Subjunctive, see Paragraph 69.

AUXILIARY VERBS.

After breakfast he WOULD (USED TO) *take a walk*	Pransus **ambulabat**
(*I*) WOULD *that you knew!*	**Vellem** } scires! **Utinam**
You SHOULD *not do this*	Non **debes** hoc facere
SHOULD *you do this you* WOULD *commit a fault* (*which I am sure you will not do*) *	Tu, si hoc **faceres**, culpam **admitteres**
I SHOULD (*be inclined to*) *think, say, &c.*	**Dixerim, crediderim,** &c.
He MUST *hear me* (*nothing shall prevent it*)	**Nihil obstabit quominus** (or **efficiam ut**) me audiat
He MUST *have seen me*	Non **potuit** me non videre
I MUST *have perished, if you had not helped me*	**Perieram,**† nisi tu mihi subvenisses
You MUST *come by way of Rome* (*for there is no other way*)	**Necesse est** per Romam venias
I MUST *obey my father*	**Oportet** me patri parere
I MUST *confess I was mistaken*	**Fatendum est** me erravisse
You MUST *know I'm at Rome*	**Scito** me Romæ esse
You MUST *not fancy you are envied*	**Noli putare** tibi invideri
LET *him return* {(1) *I beg you* (2) *if he likes*	**Permitte** homini redire **Redeat,** si velit

Rule—The Auxiliary Verbs in English being used in the Subjunctive as well as in the Indicative without change of inflection,

---

* For rules about the Tenses of the Subjunctive, see Paragraph 69.

† **Perieram** = *I had* (*assuredly*) *died*: **periissem** is more regular and common.

and having, sometimes, their original, as well as their auxiliary force, are full of ambiguities.

I OUGHT (OWED) *to* { HAVE .**Debui** } hæc facere
I COULD (WAS ABLE TO) { DONE *this* **Potui** }

Rule—After 'I ought,' 'I could,' we use the Complete Present Infinitive to denote that the action is not fulfilled. The Latins use the Present Infinitive.

The English *do* is now used in prohibitions* in order to surround the Negative as it were and annex it to the Verb, *e.g.* '*Do* not kill him.' The negative is here connected with the Verb more closely than in the older English '*kill* him *not.*' In expressing a prohibition, the Latins seem to have thought more of politeness than of directness. They did not like to say 'do not kill,' nor even, as a rule 'you will not kill,' but 'take care that you may be found hereafter not to have killed.' ' Ne **interfeceris**.'

Rule—In Latin prose a Prohibition is expressed by 'ne' with the Second Future,† or by 'noli' with the Infinitive, or 'cave ne' with the Present Subjunctive.

Ne with the Present Subjunctive is found *in poetry*, to signify prohibition.

13. The English Object was once represented by a Dative, as well as an Accusative, Inflection. In 'give *him* the book,' *him* is the Old English Dative. It would be a mistake to say that *to* is omitted before *him*. This Inflection is now lost in Nouns; but after some Verbs its place is still occasionally supplied by the Preposition *to*, e.g. 'I trust (*to*) the man.'

Some Verbs and Adjectives, though not followed by Prepositions in English, yet to a Latin ear indicated *relation to, rather than immediate action on*, the Object, *e.g.*:

* Perhaps also to *preface* the verb by an indication of prohibition or interrogation. '*Do* not come' expresses the prohibition earlier than 'come not,' and is less ambiguous than 'not come.'
† In Deponents, use Perf. Subj. 'ne aspernatus sis.'

I ENVY (LOOK ASKANCE ON) *you*   Invideo **tibi**

He is LIKE (UNTO) *his father*   Puer **patri** similis est

Rule—Verbs of trusting, pleasing, helping, hurting, yielding to, suiting, resisting, favouring, envying, being angry with, take the Dative.

Rule—Adjectives similar in meaning to the above, and also Adjectives expressing likeness or unlikeness, and proximity, also take the Dative.

<small>Instances are given in Grammars and in the examples at the end of the book. Some words signifying nearly the same thing take different cases owing to a slight difference of original meaning. Thus **medeor** meant *I am a remedy to*, and therefore takes a Dative; **sano** means *I make healthy*, and therefore takes an Accusative. So **noceo** takes a Dative, **lædo** an Accusative; **impero** *I give orders to*, a Dative, and **jubeo** *I order*, an Accusative followed by an Infinitive.</small>

Rule—Verbs signifying 'I abound in,' 'I am in need of,' 'I cease, or retire, from,' mostly take the Ablative:

Examples: **egeo, careo, abundo, vaco, desisto, cedo.** **Indigeo** mostly takes the Genitive. See Paragraphs 30, 31.

13a. Old English Impersonal and Reflexive Verbs. Several English Verbs denoting feelings that, in old times, seemed to come inexplicably upon a man from without, e.g. *pity, repent*, were once used impersonally, e.g. 'it *pitied* them,' '*it repented* him.' In the same way:—

Rule—Several Latin Verbs denoting feelings of the mind are used impersonally and govern the Genitive of the Object of the feeling, e.g. '*I repent (it repents me) of my anger*,' 'Pœnitet me iracundiæ meæ.' These verbs are **pudet, pœnitet, piget, miseret, tædet**.

Note the following :—

It is my interest that Balbus, it is the interest of Tullius that you should win the case	**Mea** interest Balbum, **Tullii** interest te judicio vincere

Rule—' Mea,' ' tua,' ' sua,' ' nostra,' ' vestra,' are used in the Feminine Ablative,* sometimes after ' interest,' and almost always after ' refert,' to denote the person to whom a matter is of importance. ' Interest ' takes the Genitive of names.

Some Verbs denoting feelings were *once* reflexive in English, *e.g.* 'he *bethought him* of.' So in Latin **misereor**, *I pity* (*me of*) ; **obliviscor**, *I forget* (*me of*) ; **reminiscor**, *I bethink*, O.E. *remember* (*myself of*), take a Genitive of the object.

He pities us	Miseretur **nostri**

Recordor, *I bear in mind*, always, and **memini** sometimes (when meaning *I keep in memory* and not *I think of*), takes the Accusative.

Several other Transitive English Verbs, *I enjoy* (*enjoy myself with*), *discharge* (*busy myself with*), *eat* (*feed myself with*), *I master* (*make myself powerful with*), are represented in Latin by Deponent Verbs governing the Ablative.

Rule—' **Fungor**,' ' **fruor**,' ' **utor**,' ' **vescor**,' ' **pascor**,' ' **potior**,'† take the Ablative.

14. The Indirect Object in English is preceded, after all but a very few Verbs, by a Preposition. *Give, ask, tell, teach, shew,* &c. are exceptions, *e.g.* 'give (to) (see page

---

* 'The origin of this singular construction is unknown. Perhaps the Pronominal Adjective has a kind of Adverbial signification, *in my direction* (*in relation to me*).'—MADVIG. It has been suggested that the original construction was ' re(m)fert Tullii, mea(m),' ' inter (rem) Tullii, mea(m) est,' abridged to the present form.

† **Potior**, like **potens**, sometimes takes the Genitive.

10) *me* the book.' In Latin (where the cases do much of the work of the English Prepositions) the indirect Object is denoted by its case.

He was keeping his father in ignorance of the deed **Patrem facinus** celabat

Rule—' Doceo,' ' celo,' ' rogo,' ' interrogo,' and ' oro,' are followed by the Accusative of the person, as the Direct Object, and also by the Accusative of the thing taught, concealed, &c. as the Indirect Object.

N.B.—Neuter Pronouns and Adjectives approximate to Adverbs, and are therefore used more freely than Masculine Pronouns and Adjectives. Note :

I advise you to do this **Hoc** te moneo

Rule—' Moneo,' ' admoneo,' and ' hortor,' take an Accusative of the Person and an Accusative of the thing, if the latter is a Neuter Pronoun.

In Elizabethan English, *banish* was used with an Indirect Object governed by an *implied* Preposition, ' I *banish* you (from) the realm.' Much more naturally could the Latins use the Indirect Object in the Accusative after the *expressed* Preposition in **transduco**, ' milites **Rhenum** transduco.'

15. Verbs implying motion. The case of the Indirect Object in Latin will be further considered under the head of Prepositions. But a few general rules may be laid down about Latin Verbs *containing Prepositions and conveying a notion of motion to, or motion from.* Such Verbs, *e.g.* **detraho**, can be used metaphorically or literally. If we say ' princeps **detrahit** milites ' we do not mean that the emperor literally himself draws away the soldiers ; but in ' **detrahit** anulum ' the Verb is literally used. *Literal* motion must be *more emphatically expressed.*

Princeps detraxit { milites **imperatori**
{ anulum **de digito suo**

Rule—Verbs containing Prepositions, and conveying a notion of motion to or from, take the Dative of the Indirect Object when not literally used.

N.B.—If literally used, they require *the Preposition to be repeated for emphasis,* as above, **detraxit de.***

Examples :—**Afferre, admovere, auferre, circumdare, circumjicere, detrahere, deripere, eripere, extorquere, imponere, imprimere, incurrere, inesse, inferre, injicere, objicere, offerre, opponere, præficere, subjicere, subjungere, supponere, subtrahere.**

Rule—Verbs signifying ' preferring ' and the contrary take the Dative of the Indirect Object, or repeat the Preposition before the Indirect Object.

Examples :—**Anteferre, anteponere, præferre, præponere, posthabere, postponere.**

16. The Object after Verbs of Motion. The Object after a Verb of *Motion to* in English sometimes dispenses with a Preposition. 'He went *home,*' 'I'm going (Early English *on,* then *a'* or *a-*) *fishing.*' Where the Preposition is not quite dispensed with, the tendency is sometimes seen, as in 'He rides *a-field.*' All Nouns that are often repeated after the same Preposition in English have a tendency to become Adverbs. Thus we say 'a-bed,' but not 'a-chair'; 'a-foot,' but not (now) 'a-knee'; 'a-sleep,' but not ' a-slumber.' Now the Romans thought more of towns, and less of countries, than we do. Farmers used at one time to live in the towns and go out to their work. So as they were *continually going into and out of their*

---

* The Dative in ' Cæsari ad pedes se projecit ' is perhaps partly Possessive, partly Dative of the Indirect Object.

homes, their fields, and their towns, but not so often into and out of countries, they omitted Prepositions before towns but retained them before countries. Small islands are naturally regarded as mere towns.

Rule—After a verb of 'motion to,' the names of towns and small islands are used in the Accusative without Prepositions, as also are 'domum,' 'humum,' and 'rus.'

Are you going A-FIELD *to-day?*   Visne **rus** hodie ire?

Rule—After a verb of 'motion from,' the names of towns and small islands are used in the Ablative without Prepositions. So are 'domo,' 'rure,' 'humo.'

We shall set out FROM *Carthage*   **Carthagine** proficiscemur

Rule—After a verb of 'rest in,' the names of towns and small islands, if singular, are in a locative case ending in -æ (which was once -ai) or -i; if plural, in the Ablative: Romæ, Corinthi, Carthagini (sometimes written Carthagine) Athenis.

The same rule holds for **domi, ruri, humi.**

The fact that **domi** and **Corinthi** are not real Genitives, explains some seeming anomalies.
You may write '**domi meæ**,' which is one notion, and '**domi Ciceronis**'; but not **domi** with an ordinary Adjective; 'in an excellent home' is '**in domo optima.**'
Urbs and **oppidum,** when in apposition to names in the locative case of the Genitive form, are placed in the Ablative, and generally (not always) preceded by **in.** '*He lived in the once populous city of Antioch.*' '**Antiochiæ, (in) celebri** quondam **urbe** vitam agebat.'

17. 'Is' used relatively. The word '*is*,' in English, sometimes means 'is relatively.' The Latins distinguish between '*is*' in 'the child *is* (in the place of) a consolation' and 'the child *is* (actually and absolutely) a boy.' In the former case they use a Dative (Representative Dative or Dative of Design) after **est**. 'Puer est mihi **solacio**,' 'Do hoc tibi **muneri**.'*

The same construction is found after one or two Latin words of *giving* and *esteeming*.

Rule—Sum, do, duco (I esteem), tribuo, take a double Dative.

This Dative, having the force of an Adjective, must not be coupled to any Adjective but one of Quantity. 'Est mihi **magno** (not **caro**) solacio.' **Magno** gives a Superlative force to the Quasi-Adjective **solacio**.

18. The Attribute. The unfortunate absence of our articles *the* and *a* compels the Latins to resort to all sorts of substitutes in the use of Adjectives. Thus they cannot translate '*the* foolish† Tullia' by 'Tullia stulta,' for that might, and indeed would, mean 'Tullia is foolish,' or 'foolish Tullia' (where foolish would be a kind of name like our '*Simple* Susan,' or like the Latin 'Africanus **Minor**,' 'Pompeius **Magnus**.') Consequently they have to find some equivalent for the defining Article. They define, by mentioning *first* the individual, and *secondly* the class with the attribute, 'Tullia, **mulier stultissima**.'

Rule—The Adjective (after 'the') qualifying the name of an individual in English, often qualifies the name of the class in Latin.

The timid *dove*   Columba, **animal timidissimum**

The‡ brave *officer* Centurio, **vir fortissimus**

19. The English use of two Adjectives. In English we often use two or more Adjectives, unconnected by Conjunctions, as epithets to a Noun, *e.g.* 'a *good, brave*

---

* Compare 'I have a king here *to* my flatterer.'—*Richard II.*
† '*Foolish*' here sometimes = 'owing to her folly.' See p. 165, IV.
‡ **Ille**,' *between the Adjective and the Noun*, sometimes = *the*.

man.' In Latin, owing partly to the absence of Articles, and partly perhaps to the allowable omission of **est,** 'vir **bonus fortis**' is inadmissible.* It might mean 'a good man is brave.' The Latins therefore insert a Conjunction, 'vir **bonus fortisque.**' In the same way the Latins do not insert ordinary Adjectives between **hic,** and the Noun qualified by **hic.** If any Adjective is inserted, it is generally **tot** or **tantus,** or some Adjective modified by **tam.** Perhaps the reason is that these Adjectives, being of a demonstrative nature, coalesce more easily with **hic.**

Do not desert me in THIS SAD *calamity*	Ne me in **hac tanta** (or **tam tristi**) calamitate deserueris

Rule—Two or more Adjectives, whether pronominal or otherwise, are not attached to the same Noun without 'et' or 'que.'

N.B.—**Ille** often comes *between* an Adjective and its Noun, 'magnus **ille** vir,' 'vir **ille** sapientissimus.'

20. 'The' defining a phrase. When a Noun is preceded by '*the*' or '*a*' and followed by a Prepositional phrase, the English must not be rendered literally in Latin. 'Homines in navi clamabant' could not convey the meaning '*the men in the ship* shouted,' but might mean 'men, *or* the men, shouted *in the ship*.' We must supply the Relative. But 'homines qui erant in navi' might mean 'men that were in.' It will therefore be better to put some Relative word *first*, and to say 'as many men as were in the ship shouted,' *i.e.* '**Quot,** or **qui** erant in navi,' or '**Quidquid hominum** erat in navi.'

Very often the ambiguity can be removed by the insertion of a Participle or Adjective. Thus, 'prælium ad Cannas multa millia hominum absumpsit,' might mean 'the battle destroyed many thousands of human beings in

---

* Where an Adjective and a Noun form one notion, *e.g.* **navis oneraria,** another Adjective, *e.g.* **maxima,** may be added.

the neighbourhood of Cannæ,' but in 'prælium ad Cannas commissum' the 'ad Cannas' is shown to be connected with commissum, by coming between the Participle and the Noun qualified by the Participle.*

Another way of removing the ambiguity is to change the Prepositional phrase into an Adjective, **prælium Cannense.**

Rule—Prepositional phrases, where a Relative is implied, require either the expression of the Relative in Latin, or the insertion of an Adjective or Participle, or else the inclusion of the Prepositional phrase between a Substantive and Adjective; *e.g.* 'Qui erant in navi,' 'Prælium **Cannense**,' 'meum erga te studium.'

There is an exception to this rule in the case of *of*. Where *of* is used for the Possessive Inflection *'s*, it is rendered by the Latin Genitive. See also Paragraph 33 for other exceptions.

21. Other uses of 'the' that require notice (73) are:—

I am not THE *man to do thus*	Non is sum qui hoc faciam
He was THE *first to rise*	Ille **primus surrexit**
THE † *sooner*, THE *better*	**Quo** citius, **eo** melius

The, when meaning *the great*, requires care, *e.g.* 'I perceived *the* kindness with which I was welcomed by Tullius.' If you translate this 'Intellexi benevolentiam, quacum me Tullius excepit,' the meaning is, 'I perceived kindness, with which,' &c. But the object of *perceived* is, not really *kindness*, but the *whole of the phrase defined by* '*the*.' This can only be expressed in Latin by using a dependent interrogative form that shall shew that the

* Such expressions as **prælium ad Cannas, epistola ad Balbum (data)**, though they sometimes occur, are to be avoided.
† In Early English *thi* was used as the Ablative of the Demonstrative and of the Relative, **quo ... eo**. See *Shakespearian Grammar*, Par. 94.

object of **intellexi** is, not **benevolentiam**, but '**quanta me benevolentia Tullius exciperet.**' See Paragraph 53.

22. '**A**,' '**no**,' '**every**.' *A* is generally unexpressed: but, if it means '*a certain*' as in '*a* man once said to me,' it is sometimes translated by **quidam**.

Carefully distinguish between, on the one hand, *a* referring to a class—'*a* high tree, **arbor** (-es) **alta** (-æ), is more exposed to lightning than *a* low one'—and, on the other hand, *a* when referring to an individual of that class: '*a* tall tree (**alta quædam** arbor) stood in my garden.' Often *a* approximates to *a kind of*, e.g. '*a* curious torpor,' '**mira quædam** inertia.'

No when applied to persons, e.g. '*no* poet,' must be rendered by **nemo** (**ne homo**) (not by **nullus**), *e.g.* '**nemo poeta**,' *i.e.* 'no man, provided that he is a poet.'

Every must not be rendered by **omnis** (which generally means *all*) but by **omnes**, or, with Superlatives, by **quisque**. The Superlative, being regarded as a Noun and emphatic, comes first, '**doctissimus quisque.**'

23. English Present Participles are freely used as Adjectives. We speak of '*a degrading, humiliating, perplexing, pleasing, amusing, annoying* state of things. The preceding *a* or *the* enables us thus easily to convert Participles into Adjectives. The Latins, not having the Articles, have not the same converting facility.

Rule—Present Participles must not be used as Adjectives in Latin unless the use is established by authority, as 'sapiens.'

Adjectives must be used instead, *e.g.* **turpis** for *degrading:* or the sentence may be turned so as to use a Verb.

24. Adverbs and Adverbial phrases in English are very often compounded with Prepositions, e.g. *a-foot*, *a-main*, *at home*, *in haste*, *with anger*, *by right*, *of course*. In such phrases, *with* is the most common Preposition, and it is therefore useful to remember the following:—

Rule—'With' must not be translated by the simple Ablative unless it denotes instrumentality.

E.g. 'He struck me *with* a stick,' '**Baculo** me percussit: but 'He answered *with* impetuosity, '**Vehementer** respondit;' or '**Cum vehementia** respondit.'

N.B.—If an Adjective comes between *with* and its Substantive, *e.g.* 'with *great* impetuosity,' the Ablative may be used: '**summa** vehementia.'

There are all degrees of any quality, *e.g.* **celeritas**. The Abl. in '**celeritate** adiit' is felt not to define the manner: for the question arises '*with what* speed?' But join **summa** to it, and we get an Adverbial expression *defining the manner*. The English 'with speed,' means '**with** (great) speed.'

Rule—'In,' when used metaphorically in English, must not be rendered by 'in' in Latin.

E.g. *in time* meaning *at last*, is **tandem**, or, meaning *punctuality*, is **tempori**; *in haste* is **celeriter**, or **summa celeritate** (but not **celeritate**). *In* my *opinion* is **me judice**.

In, meaning *in the case of*, is sometimes found in Latin used metaphorically: **in Themistocle**, *in the case of Themistocles*.
The following Ablatives are regarded as Adverbs and do not require Adjectives. *In due course*, recte atque **ordine**; *methodically*, **via et ratione**; *in word*, **verbo**; *in appearance*, **specie**; *in reality*, **re**, or **re ipsa**; *rightly*, **jure**; *not unnaturally*, neque **injuria**; *with force*, **vi**; *with craft*, **dolo**. There are other exceptions that should not be used by beginners.

25. Adverbs. The following Adverbs require care. *Now* sometimes means *at the present moment:* in that case it is in Latin **nunc**. Sometimes it means *by this time*, **or** *already:* in that case it is **jam**.

[Par. 25.] **ADVERBS.** 21

I have been waiting for NOW *three days*	**Jam** triduum expecto
Can you see me NOW ?	Num me **nunc** videre potes ?

Rule—'Nunc' applies to the Present simply; 'jam' to the Present considered with reference to the Past or Future, *i.e.* after past waiting, *by this time*, or, before it was expected, *already*.

Only sometimes expresses something less than was expected: 'he *only* spoke; he did nothing.' In these cases use **tantum**. Where *only* means *by himself, by itself*, use **solus (m)**.* 'Not *only*' is almost always 'non **solum**,' or 'non **modo**.' In 'if *only*,' 'provided *only*,' the Latins use **modo**. Sometimes *only* is to be expressed by **nihil aliud quam**. 'In his old age, instead of riding he *only* walked,' 'Senex, omissa equitatione, **nihil aliud quam** deambulabat.'

More, when used with verbs and meaning *to a greater extent*, is **plus**; when used with Adjectives, and also when meaning *rather*, it is **magis**.

I love him MORE *than his brother*	Amo illum **plus** quam fratrem ejus
He is MORE *dutiful to his father than you are*	Ille **magis** est quam tu erga patrem pius †
I hope MORE (RATHER) *than fear*	**Magis** spero quam timeo

With numbers, use **supra** as Preposition or **amplius** See Paragraph 41, '*Above*.'

Note the curious construction :

He was MORE *foolhardy than bold*	**Audacior** erat quam **fortior**

* In this case, *alone* is preferable to *only*.
† Adjectives ending in **-eus, -ius,** and others that do not take the Comparative in **-ior,** take **magis** instead of the termination.

Once is (1) **forte**, *once upon a time;* (2) **semel**, *once for all;* (3) **quondam** or **olim**, *formerly.*

26. The Prepositions in English do the work, not only of the Latin Prepositions, but also of many of the Latin cases, and (as will be seen hereafter) of many of the Latin Conjunctions. Consequently, in translating them into Latin, they require especial care. Distinguish always between the original *local* meaning of a Preposition and its subsequent *metaphorical* meaning. Thus *of* or *off* originally meant *motion from:* in Early English we find 'the leaves fall *of* (*off*) the tree.' Later, the purely *local* meaning of *motion from* was used to express an action that proceeded *from* the agent, 'we were received *of** (*by*) the most pious Edward.' Lastly, coming to mean connection of any kind, *of* was used of anything, not proceeding from, but *belonging to,* anyone, *e.g.* 'the misfortunes *of* this worthy man.'

It is evident that the same notion, e.g. *agency* or *price,* may be represented by a different Preposition according as the notion is regarded. Thus, an action may be regarded as coming *out of* the agent; in that case we may use *of,* as in Elizabethan English. But it may also be regarded as *near,* i.e. by (*by* originally meant *near*), the agent. So price may be represented by *at,* denoting neighbourhood and hence equivalence, or *for* denoting (1) *standing before,* or *in the place of,* and hence (2) equivalence ; or in certain context you may say 'I bought it *with* my last shilling,' treating it as an ordinary action performed *with,* i.e. *near,* the instrument.

The differences in Prepositions are so slight that they vary with the slightest variety of context; and some Prepositions that were in fashion during one period pass out of fashion in another. Thus we cannot now say as Shakespeare did, 'I live *with* bread,' 'he died *with* tickling,' but *with* after 'disagree' is not yet entirely supplanted by *from.*

This being the case, before going through all the idioms

* *Macbeth*, iii. 6. 27.

connected with the several Prepositions, we should go at once to the *notions* represented by the Prepositions, and consider how those *notions* are to be represented. In a language like the Latin, abounding in cases, the Prepositions have not been so much used as in English, and have consequently *not so often assumed metaphorical meanings*. They are mostly used locally; the metaphorical English Prepositions are mostly represented by the Latin cases.

27. Extension. *For* means sometimes *as an equivalent for* (one thing standing in the front of, i.e. *in the stead of*, another): *e.g.* '**Pro** tantis tuis meritis, quid tibi dabo?' sometimes *on account of*, **ob** or **propter**; sometimes, from its meaning *of equivalence*, it is used almost redundantly to mean *as much as* before time and space, *e.g.* 'he walked *for* five miles,' 'he waited *for* ten minutes.' The Latins do not use (nor do the English always) a redundant Preposition here, but put the noun in the Accusative as a kind of Object after the Verb, *e.g.* 'Tridui **iter** processimus,' 'Decem jam **dies** hic moramur.' The *for* is omitted with the Adjectives *long, broad, deep, high,* ' Hasta sex **pedes** longa,' ' Fossa decem **pedes** alta.'

Rule—Extension of time and space is expressed by the Accusative.

For, before time, when followed by a negative—e.g. '*For* the last ten years he never came '—is not expressed by the Accusative. The notion of *extension* seemed to the Latins lost, as there was *no action going on during the time*; and the meaning seemed to be '*within* ten years.' The Latins therefore used (see 28) the Ablative: '**Decem annis** Romam non venit.' Often **his,** i.e. '*last*,' is added: 'Nemo **his decem annis** talia ausus est.'

28. Point of time. *At, in, by* (all denoting neighbourhood) are used in English to denote the time when a thing is done. In Latin the Ablative (which expresses a *circumstance* *) is naturally used to denote this.

* "The Ablative denotes in general that a thing belongs to the predicate as serving to complete and define it more accurately (so that it stands with the thing predicated in the relation of an *appurtenance* or *circumstance*).'— MADVIG's *Latin Grammar.*

'**Tertio anno** urbs capta est,' 'Saturni stella **triginta** fere **annis** cursum suum conficit.'

Rule—The Ablative denotes the time at which or within which anything is completed.

At, of place, must be expressed by **ad** or **in**, not by the Ablative by itself; '**ad** hunc locum,' 'hoc **in** loco;' not 'hoc loco.'

Hieme, æstate, die, nocte, luce, are also used for the *season within which* anything is done—'*in* winter,' '*by* day,' &c.

29. Price is expressed in English indefinitely by *at*, definitely by *for* or (rarely) by *with*. The English *at* (perhaps representing contiguity) is expressed by the Latin Genitive, perhaps the Genitive of quality.* The Latins do not use **pro** to denote price. *For* and *with* (instrumental) are represented by the Latin Ablative (denoting a circumstance, see Paragraph 28, Note). It would seem that price when *indefinite* (as it is when you ask how much a man will offer) is regarded by the Latins as a quality, and expressed by the Genitive; when *definite*, it is regarded as an instrument and expressed by the Ablative. '*At* what price did you buy the rice?' 'Oh, *for* a small sum.' '**Quanti** oryza empta est?' '**Parvo.**'

Rule—The price is expressed by the Ablative.

Rule—Tanti, quanti, pluris, minoris (but magno, parvo, plurimo, &c.) are used after verbs of *selling* and *buying*.

Rule—Magni, pluris, plurimi, parvi, minoris, minimi, tanti, quanti, and nihili are used after *verbs of estimation*, and after est signifying *it is worth*.

This seems to be a kind of Genitive of quality. The same construction, after **non æstimo, facio,** &c. is used with **assis, flocci,** &c. 'Non te **flocci** facio,' 'I don't value you at a straw.'

* Madvig says, "This Genitive is nearly allied to the Descriptive Genitive."

30. Fulness, in English, is generally expressed by Verbs and Adjectives followed by *of* or *with*. *Of* denotes that the *fulness* arises *out of* something; *with*, that the fulness is connected *with* something. *Of* is represented by the Latin Genitive, which in the best authors follows **plenus**. *With* (or *in*, e.g. 'abounds *in*') is represented by the Latin Ablative, which naturally follows Verbs, *e.g.* **compleo** and **impleo**, to express the *instrument* by which the state of fulness denoted by the Verb is brought about.

Rule—Adjectives, as well as Verbs, expressing fulness are followed by the Genitive or Ablative.

See Paragraph 13.

31. Emptiness is generally expressed in English by *of* or *from*, 'void *of*,' 'free *from*.' *Of* denotes *motion of* (*off*) and then *connection*, 'as regards'; *from* denotes more distinctly *motion from*. Hence, in Latin, the Genitive is used where *connection*, *motion in search of*, *need of*, is denoted; and the Ablative (which represents an external circumstance *) is used where *motion* or *absence from* is denoted. Thus 'I have need *of* money' is 'Egeo pecuniæ,' but 'I am destitute *of*, i.e. without money,' is 'Careo pecunia.'

Rule—Adjectives and Verbs denoting emptiness are followed by the Genitive or Ablative.

(1) **Inops, pauper, egenus, indigus**, and **parcus** take the Genitive. (2) **Inanis, nudus, orbus, vacuus, liber, immunis, purus** (*clean from*), **extorris** and **alienus** (which last is generally followed by **ab**), take the Ablative; so also do the verbs **spolio, abstineo, libero, solvo, levo, exonero, arceo, prohibeo**, take the Ablative of the thing.

32. English Prepositions following Adjectives may often be rendered by the Latin Ablative. The reason for

* See Paragraph 28, Note.

this is, that many Adjectives, having the force of Participles and describing a state, naturally take the Ablative to denote the *instrument* producing the state. Thus 'relying *on* your help' is '**fretus** (supported by) **tuo** auxilio'; 'heavy *with* gold,' '**onustus** (laden with) **auro**.' So with **præditus** and **contentus**. In the following rule the Adjectives have not the force of Participles; the Ablative rather expresses a circumstance, 'dignus **mercede**,' 'worthy *in point of* pay.'

Rule—' Dignus ' and ' indignus ' take the Ablative.

Of in 'born *of* obscure parents' has its radical meaning *off* or *from*. It is therefore naturally represented by the Ablative in Latin.

Rule—'Natus,' 'satus,' ' ortus,' ' genitus,' ' editus,' take the Ablative.

33. **A Preposition between two Nouns** in English often denotes that the second is the object of an action implied by the first, *e.g.* (1) 'hunger *for* gold,' (2) 'experience *in* warfare,' (3) 'incitement *to* danger,' (4) 'rules *about* life,' (5) 'exemption *from* warfare.' In a great number of these cases, the English Preposition might be replaced by *as regards*. Now this *as regards* is one of the radical meanings not only of the English *of*, but also of the Latin Genitive. Consequently this Objective relation, *as regards*, is expressed in Latin by the Genitive, *e.g.* (1) '**Auri** fames,' (2) ' **Rei militaris** peritia,' (3) ' **Periculi** incitamentum,' (4) ' **Vitæ** præcepta,' (5) ' **Militiæ** vacatio.'

This is called the Objective Genitive.

Rule—A Preposition (often ' of ' or ' for ') between two Nouns, if it denotes that the second is the Object of the first, is often expressed by the Latin Genitive.

The Genitive is hence sometimes ambiguous: *e.g.* 'Injuriæ **Æduorum**' may mean 'injuries done *by*, or done *to*, the Ædui.'

34. 'Of' after a Participial Adjective, formed from a Transitive Verb, is found, though not often, in English, *e.g.* 'I *spare* my purse,' 'he is *sparing of* his purse.' The fact is, *sparing* is here a kind of noun, and the construction is the same as* in 'he is a niggard *of* his money.' This *of*, meaning *as regards*, is rendered in Latin by the Genitive, and such Participial Adjectives often occur in Latin where there are no corresponding Participial Adjectives in English.

Rule—(1) Latin Active Present Participles from Transitive Verbs, when used as Adjectives, and (2) Adjectives in -ax, from Transitive Verbs, take the Genitive, *e.g.* 'Laborum patiens.'

So **amans, capax, edax, tenax, prudens, insolens, potens,**† **impotens.**

35. 'Of' and 'in' after several other Adjectives in English are used in the sense of 'as regards.' These Adjectives *suggest an object:* e.g. 'he is greedy' suggests the question 'he is greedy as regards what?' Such Adjectives mostly express *desire, experience* or *inexperience, knowledge* or *ignorance, participation, guilt, innocence,*

---

* Unless it is a result of the genuine Old English (still preserved in the slang of London and perhaps of other places), 'he is a-sparing (in *or* on sparing) *of* his purse.' Compare 'the shepherd blowing *of* his nails,' 3 *Henry VI.* ii. 5. 3.—*Shakespearian Grammar*, Paragraph 178.

† Many Genitives after Adjectives may be explained by saying that the Adjective implies a Verb and Noun, which Noun naturally governs the Genitive. Thus **potens** means *having power of*. Compare
'The sovereign *power* you have *of* us.'—*Hamlet*, ii. 2. 27.
So, in Greek. λύπης ἀμοιρός ἐστι means οὐκ ἔχει μοῖραν λύπης.

e.g. 'inexperienced *in* treachery,' 'greedy *of* praise.' These Prepositions are rendered by the Latin Genitive, which naturally expresses the connection implied in *as regards*.

Rule—An English Preposition between an Adjective and a Noun, when denoting that the Noun is the object of the Adjective, is often rendered by the Latin Genitive, *e.g.* 'Avidus laudis,' 'Perfidiæ imperitus.'

So, **avarus, cupidus, conscius, inscius, nescius, rudis, gnarus, ignarus, peritus, memor, immemor, particeps, expers** (also Abl.), **reus, insons**.

36. '**Of**' after the Verbs **accuse, acquit,** but not after *condemn*, is used in English in the sense of *as regards, about*. In Latin the Genitive, which answers to this use of *of*, is more common. But as these verbs are also used with the Instrumental Ablative **crimine** followed by the Genitive of the charge, it is possible that the Genitive depends on **crimine** understood.

Rule—'Accuso,' 'incuso,' 'insimulo,' 'arguo,' 'convinco,' 'damno,' 'condemno,' 'absolvo,' take the Genitive of the charge.

37. '**Of**' preceding a **Noun denoting quality.** *Of* meaning *out of* is naturally placed before the material (*out*) *of* which anything is made, and hence before the *qualities that go to make up anything*. This use of *of* is rendered, when referring to literal construction, by an Adjective, *e.g.* **marmoreus,** or by **de** or **e**, *e.g.* 'factum **de** or **e marmore**;' but, when metaphorical, by the Latin Genitive of Quality, *e.g.* 'he is a man *of* honour,' 'summæ est **integritatis,**' 'it is a matter *of* difficulty,' '**res est multi laboris.**' The Ablative (denoting circum-

stance) can also be thus used : 'vir est **summa integritate**.'

N.B.—Do not omit the *Adjective*, e.g. write '**summæ** (-a) integritatis (-e),' not 'integritatis (-e)' alone.

The reason for the insertion of the Adjective seems to be this: 'puer **naso,** *or* **oris** est' contains no definition, as all boys have noses and faces; but 'naso **adunco**,' 'oris **pulcri**,' imply definition. The Adjective, though omitted in English, is really implied, 'he is a man *of (great) ability*.'

Rule—*Of* preceding a Noun of quality is rendered in Latin by a Genitive or Ablative.

38. Of (*out of*, that which *comes from*, and hence *belongs to*, anyone) is often preceded by 'the mark' to express a characteristic, *e.g.* 'it is *the mark of* a philosopher to be cautious.' Sometimes we omit 'the mark;' we cannot however venture to say 'it is *of* a philosopher,' but we sometimes, especially after a negative, say 'it is not *like* a philosopher to chatter.' The Latins can use the Genitive as a Predicate in all such cases, and can say '**Philosophi cavere est,** *or* non est garrire.'

Rule—*It is the mark of, It is like*, are often expressed by the Latin Genitive.

39. Prepositions implying rest or motion. When an action or state is described, the English generally express by Prepositions the place *where* the action takes place. On the other hand, the Latins (and Greeks) usually express the place *whence* the action originates, or *whither* it is directed.

This is ON *my side*	Hoc **a** me facit
ON *the south-west and north-east*	**Ab** occasu æstivo, et **ab** ortu hiberno
The fruit was hanging ON *the trees*	Pendebat **ex** arboribus fructus

He came from (to) his home AT Corinth	Corintho (-um), domo (-um) sua* (-m) venit
ON *our way we broke down the bridge*	Ex itinere pontem exscidimus
But, ON *our way the enemy attacked us*	Hostis nos in itinere oppressit (*rare*)

Rule—English Prepositions denoting rest must often be rendered by Latin Prepositions denoting motion.

40. The redundant 'of.' *Of* (partitive) is naturally used in such phrases as 'ten (*out*) *of* twenty;' but it has come to be loosely used, by false analogy, after *all*, in 'all *of* us' and after a number *that does not represent a part* but a whole, *e.g.* 'three hundred *of* us came.' The Latins do not adopt this erroneous construction, but say '**nos omnes, nos trecenti** venimus.' A similar redundant *of* is often used between 'town' or 'city,' and the particular name of the town or city, *e.g.* 'the city *of* London.' This is not found in Latin: 'urbs **Londinium.**'

Rule—Do not translate into Latin the redundant '*of*.'

Of is often used after abstract Nouns, and sometimes ambiguously, *e.g.* "the reminiscences *of* (? *by* or *about*) Balbus." The Latins dislike ambiguity and (3 *a*) abstract Nouns. Hence:—

The top OF *the mountain*	**Summus mons**
The rest OF *the ships*	**Reliquæ naves**

After *Before*	the foundation OF the city the capture OF the soldiers the birth OF Tullius sun-rise	Post Ante	urbem conditam milites captos Tullium natum solem ortum

* The anomalous **domum, -i,** &c. may be qualified by a Genitive or by a Possessive Adjective, but by no other Adjective. See Par. 16.

Rule—The Latins often avoid the ambiguous Genitive and the use of abstract Nouns, by using an Adjective or Participle instead of a Noun in the Genitive, followed by another Noun.

41. Dictionary of Prepositions. The following Preposition-idioms will serve to illustrate the difference between the English and Latin Prepositions. Prepositions used as Conjunctions, e.g. '*before* he could arrive,' and followed by Verbals, e.g. '*before* leaving,' are reserved for Paragraphs 66, 75.

The student will not fail to notice the large number of compound Prepositions having no corresponding Prepositions in Latin, and therefore requiring to be rendered in some other form.

About (*external neighbourhood*; *á-be-out*).

ABOUT *noon*, 8 A.M. *&c.*	**Circiter** / **Circa** } meridiem, secundam horam
ABOUT (TOWARDS, COMING UP TO, GETTING ON FOR) *nightfall*	**Ad,** better **sub,** noctem
ABOUT (DURING, BEFORE THE END OF, TAKING A PART OUT OF) *night*	**De** nocte surrexit

Above (radical meaning, *position over, a-be-ove,* where *ove* is connected with *over* and *up*); (1) *above,* with notion of motion, **super ;** (2) with notion of rest, **supra ;** (3) *above,* figuratively, **supra.**

This is ABOVE *my strength*	Hoc **supra** vires est
ABOVE 500 *men were slain*	**Super** (or **supra**) quingentos (or Quingenti **amplius**) occisi sunt.
He is ABOVE *deceit*	Honestior est quam qui mentiatur

According to.

ACCORDING TO *Herodotus, the facts are somewhat different*	**Herodoto teste** res aliter se habet
They will be rewarded ACCORDING TO *their deeds*	Suam quisque **pro** factis mercedem accipient

After (aft-er).

When one event comes immediately *after* another, it may be regarded as coming *out of it*. Indeed *after* is derived from *of*, 'a comparative formed from *of*' (Morris), and may therefore naturally be rendered by *out of*, which is an emphatic way of expressing *of*. Hence, beside the more usual **post :**

Immediately AFTER *his consulship he left Rome*	**Ex** consulatu Româ excessit
One thing AFTER (ON THE HEELS OF) *another*	Aliud **ex** alio me turbat
He waited day AFTER *day*	Diem **ex** die expectabat
AFTER *your letter they read mine*	**Sub** (*following from below*) tuas literas, statim recitabant meas
AFTER (FOLLOWING ON, BUT NOT IMMEDIATELY) *this battle*	**Secundum** (*rare*) hanc pugnam.
The day AFTER *the battle*	**Postridie pugnam**
AFTER (NEXT TO) *God, you are my hope*	**Secundum** Deos, in te spem pono
AFTER (COMING CLOSE TO) *the manner of a battle*	**Ad** similitudinem pugnæ milites sese exercebant
AFTER *the manner of slaves*	**Ad** modum servorum

Against (1) when preceded by a verb of motion is often rendered by Latin, **in**, *e.g.* ' Incitare **in** ;' (2) when meaning 'in opposition to,' by **contra,** ' Conjurant **contra** rempublicam;' (3) when meaning active hostility, by **adversus,** 'Adversus te contendimus.'

Agreeably to (i.e. *in agreement with*).

Are you acting AGREEABLY TO *your orders in loitering here?*	Num **ad** (*up to*) præscriptum agis, hic tempus terens?
We ought to live AGREEABLY TO *nature*	Naturæ **convenienter** vivendum est
We will speak AS AGREEABLY *as possible to the truth*	Dicemus quam maxime **ad** veritatem **accommodate**

Among (*mixed with*). (1) Of nations and large societies, **apud**; (2) meaning *in the number of*, **in**; (3) meaning *conspicuous amid*, **inter**; (4) meaning *selected from among*, **e**; (5) after a verb of motion, literal or metaphorical, sometimes **in**.

AMONG *the Germans*	**Apud** Germanos
Pain is reckoned AMONG *the most serious evils*	Dolor **in** maximis malis ducitur
A battle memorable AMONG *the few defeats of the Roman people*	Pugna memorata **inter** paucas Romanorum clades
He was the only one AMONG *seven that lived to manhood*	Unus **e** septem togam virilem sumpsit
I will divide the booty AMONG *my companions*	Prædam **in** socios distribuam

Around, see **Round.**

As for, as regards, as to, when at the beginning of the sentence, may be rendered by **Quantum** (or **quod**) **attinet ad**; when in the middle, by **de** (*concerning*).

D

At (neighbourhood).

AT *the mercy of Balbus*	**In manu** *or* **potestate** Balbi
The city is AT *the mercy of fire*	Urbs incendiis est **obnoxia***
AT (*i.e.* CLOSE TO *or* FOLLOWING ON) *this*	**Sub** or **ad** hæc
*I aim-*AT, *laugh-*AT, *look-*AT, *you*	Te **peto, rideo, specto**

N.B.—Not '**miror** te,' unless you mean 'I admire you.' Better 'admirationem mihi moves,' if you mean 'I am surprised AT you.'

AT THE BEGINNING OF } *the battle*	**Incipiente** } jam pugna
AT THE END OF	**Finem capiente**
He is AT THE POINT OF *death*	**In eo est ut** moriatur

Before (in the *fore* part) : (1) generally **ante**, after verbs both of rest and motion ; (2) **præ** after verbs of motion, *immediately in front of*, often used in the phrase **præ se** ; (3) **pro**, *rest in front of;* (4) **ob**, motion *to meet, to the face of;* (5) **apud**, more rarely **ad**, *in the presence of* (*a body of people*) ; (6) **coram**, *in the presence of* (*an individual*), *face to face with*.

When *before* is applied metaphorically to (7) time, **ante** is used ; when to (8) *preference*, **ante**, or (rarely) **præ**.

He sent the cavalry BEFORE *him*	Equitatum **ante** se misit (but, **præmisit**)
He held a dagger BEFORE *him*	Pugionem **præ** se tulit
They were on guard BEFORE *the gate*	**Pro** portis in statione erant
Death presents itself BEFORE *our eyes*	Mors **ob** oculos versatur

* Tacitus, but not Cicero.

He was brought to trial BEFORE *the jury*	**Apud** judices reus factus est
He said this BEFORE *the king*	**Coram** rege hæc dixit
Ten years BEFORE *the consulship of Balbus*	Decimo anno **ante** Balbum Consulem
Balbus was BEFORE *all in military distinction*	Balbus **ante** alios in re militari floruit

Below
Beneath } **infra,** literally and metaphorically.

This is BENEATH *me*	Hoc est **infra** me

Below is often to be rendered by **indignus est,** or **turpior est,** *e.g.*:

He is BENEATH *your notice*	**Turpior est quam** ut debeas illi irasci (or **quam cui**)

Beside.

This is BESIDE *the mark*	Hoc est **nihil ad rem,** or **proposito alienum**
He is BESIDE *himself*	**Non** est apud se

Besides, when meaning in *addition to,* **præter;** but 'Besides this there was &c.' is often rendered '**Huc accedebat ut** esset &c.'

Beyond: (1) of space and time, **ultra;** with motion, sometimes **præter;** (2) outside, **extra;** (3) metaphorically, *exceeding,* **supra.**

The lake had swollen BEYOND *its limits*	Lacus **præter** modum creverat
This is BEYOND *belief*	Hoc **supra** fidem est
BEYOND *question*	**Sine** ulla dubitatione

But (connected with *out; leaving out*), **præter**. After a negative, or a question implying a negative, this Preposition is sometimes replaced by the Conjunction **nisi**.

What else was history then, BUT *mere annal-writing?*	Quid tum erat historia **nisi** (*if it was not*) annalium confectio?
He ALL BUT (EVERYTHING EXCEPT) *took the city*	Urbem **tantum non** (*just so much as not*) cepit

By (*neighbourhood,* hence *agency, cause, instrumentality*).

I have a garden BY *the Tiber*	**Ad** (place) Tiberim hortum habeo
I was sitting BY *Balbus*	**Apud** (person) Balbum sedebam
We travelled BY SEA, *but the journey is mostly performed* BY *land*	**In navi** vecti sumus; iter autem plerique **pedibus** conficiunt
Whenever he was BY HIMSELF	Quoties **solus** erat
He did it BY HIMSELF	**Ipse, nullis adjuvantibus**, hoc fecit
I shall return BY (*my return is fixed* FOR, *so as to come up* TO) *the thirteenth of April*	**Ad** Idus Apriles redibo

By signifying *agency* is rendered by **a** or **ab** to denote that the action comes from the agent; signifying *instrumentality*, by the Ablative, which denotes a circumstance, and therefore, among others, the *instrument*; signifying a *medium*, a *remote instrument*, by **per**.

I was informed BY *letter,* BY *spies, &c.*	**Per** literas, exploratores, certior factus sum
BY *stealth, craft, degrees*	**Furtim, dolo, paulatin**

If not BY *fair means, then* BY *foul*	Si possis **recte** ; sin minus, **quocunque modo**
Ireland is less BY (INSTRUMENTALITY) *a half than Britain*	Hibernia **dimidio** minor est quam Britannia
Day BY (FOLLOWING ON) *day; one* BY *one*	**In dies ; singuli**
BY (*in the presence of*) *Heaven!*	{ **Proh** deum atque hominum fidem ! **Hercle !**
BY (*according to*) *what you say, there is no hope*	**Hæc si vera dicis**, spes nulla restat
BY WAY OF *showing his gratitude, he gave me this present*	Hoc mihi donum dedit, **quippe** grati in me animi **documentum**

Rule—'By' signifying agency must be followed by 'a' or 'ab' with the Ablative.

Concerning, de, presents no difficulty.

Considering.

He was well read, CONSIDERING *his youth,* or AS BOYS GO	Multæ erant, **ut (dicam)** in puero literæ, *or* **ut est captus puerorum**
CONSIDERING (IN PROPORTION TO) *our numbers, our country is small*	Fines, **pro** multitudine nostra, angustos habemus

During: (1) *all through, in the course of,* **per**; (2) *in the midst of,* **inter** ; (3) *in,* **in** (rare) ; (4) often rendered by **dum**, or by an Absolute Ablative.

DURING *three years, he used to read* DURING *his dinner*	**Per** triennum, **inter** cœnam legebat
DURING *the night he saw a dragon*	**Secundum** or **per** quietem (but also **in quiete**) visus ei draco
DURING *the reign of Tullius*	**Tullio** rege
He used to walk DURING *his sleep*	**Dormiens** ambulabat

Except (præter with acc.).

Where *except* is followed by *that*, or by a Preposition, it really governs a phrase and is a *Conjunction*, not a Preposition. It is then to be rendered by (1) **præterquam**, or (after a negative expressed or implied in a question expecting a negative answer), by (2) **nisi**.

I am charmed by my estate, EXCEPT THAT *it is not fertile enough*	Prædia valde me delectant, **nisi** quod parum fertilia sunt
I sent no letter EXCEPT TO *you*	Nullas literas **præterquam** *or* **nisi** ad te misi
WITH THE EXCEPTION OF *one or at most two*	**Excepto** uno aut ad summum altero

Excluding, exclusive of.

EXCLUSIVE OF (BESIDES) *his personal property, he has large estates*	**Præter** pecunias, prædia magna habet
EXCLUSIVE OF (*not to speak of*) *faults, he has committed shameful crimes*	Flagitia, **nedum** *or* **ne dicam**, culpas admisit

For, radical meaning *in front of*: hence (1) *in place* (*stead*) *of*; (2) *in behalf of*; (3) *for the sake of*; (4) *regard* being had to; (5) because of; (6) for the purpose of; (7) with a view to; (8) as good as; (9) as much (long) as; (10) for the price of; (11) for what concerns; (12) about.

They use shells FOR (INSTEAD OF) money	**Pro** nummo conchis utuntur
He exchanges honour FOR money	Argentum **fama** mutat, i.e. 'buys with fame'
We must fight FOR (IN BEHALF OF) our country	**Pro** patria dimicandum est
I fear FOR you, not FOR myself	**Tibi** non **mihi** timeo. (rare)
FOR heaven's SAKE, help me!	**Per** te deos oro ut mihi subvenias
The battle was sanguinary FOR (REGARD BEING HAD TO) the number of the combatants	Prælium atrocius erat quam (æquum erat expectare) **pro** numero pugnantium
I cannot speak FOR (BECAUSE OF) joy	**Præ** gaudio nequeo eloqui. (After a negative.)
He took a bribe FOR deciding a suit	**Ob** rem judicandam pecuniam accepit

Also in this last sense, **propter** and **de**.

He had been selected FOR (FOR THE PURPOSE OF) the contest, which had been fixed FOR (WITH A VIEW TO, LOOKING FORWARD TO) the following day	**In** certamen electus erat, quod **in** posterum diem constitutum erat. (After a Verb of motion, real or metaphorical.)
I will set out FOR Athens	Athenas proficiscar
I will wait FOR THE PRESENT, or, if you wish, FOR A LONGER TIME	**In** præsens vel, si posces, **diutius** expectabo

This will serve FOR (AS GOOD AS) *an example to us*	Hoc nobis exemplo erit. (See Par. 17.)
He waited at first FOR (AS MUCH AS) *ten days, then* FOR (LONG DURATION) *two whole years*	Homo primum decem **dies**, postea **per** biennium expectabat. (See Par. 27.)
FOR *how much did you buy this?* FOR *a small sum*	**Quanti** hoc emisti? **Parvo.** (See Par. 29.)
FOR (FOR WHAT CONCERNS) *my part, I shall go away*	**Equidem** abibo
We are badly off FOR *provisions*	**A** re frumentaria laboramus
As FOR (FOR WHAT CONCERNS) *the prisoners, I know nothing about them*	**Quod** attinet ad **captivos**, *or*, **De captivis**, nihil habeo compertum
FOR *beauty she excels them all*	Mulier, **pulcritudine** (Instr.) quidem, *or* **quantum ad pulcritudinem** facile est princeps
FOR (FOR WHAT CONCERNS) *success he is too slothful*	**Ignavior** est quam qui *or* quam ut possit rem bene gerere
He is too hasty FOR (FOR WHAT CONCERNS) *me*	**Vehementior** est quam qui *or* quam ut possit mihi placere
He was too late FOR *the* DINNER	**Serius** advenit **quam ut posset** e convivis esse
There is no cause FOR *despair*	Non est **cur desperes**
He may die FOR (FOR WHAT CONCERNS) *me*	**Per** me licet pereat

FOR (FOR WHAT CONCERNS) *all I know*	**Quod sciam**
FOR (AS FAR AS REGARDS, IN SPITE OF) *all you say, you will not persuade me*	**Quodcunque** (*or* **Quamvis multa**) dixeris, non mihi persuadebis
I am FOR *Tullius*	Equidem **Tullio studeo**
You are no match FOR *him*	Scito te esse **illi** imparem
So much FOR (ABOUT) *this subject*	**De** hac re hactenus

For .... to. *For* was once used before *to* as a sign of the infinitive, used in the sense of purpose, *e.g.* 'What went ye out *for to* see?' Hence sometimes, where *for* is apparently a Preposition governing a Noun, it is really connected with *to*, and perhaps should be considered as governing the whole of the following clause, *e.g.* 'The wind sits fair* *for news to go*, i.e. *for the going of news*, to Ireland,' '**ad perferendum nuntium.**'

This use of *for* is especially common after *too*, 'He is too deceitful *for* me to believe him.' Here *for* is not to be taken with *me*, but with *me-to-believe*, i.e. 'for the purpose of making me believe, he is too deceitful.' This the Latins render thus : ' he is more deceitful than anyone that I should believe :' 'Hic est **fallacior quam cui** equidem credam.' (See Par. 73.)

Sometimes there is no notion of purpose, as in 'it is rare *for*,' 'it is common *for*,' in which cases the Latins would generally turn the sentence by the Adverbs '**raro**,' '**saepe**,' sometimes by **fit ut**.

It is rare FOR *him to commit a fault*	**Raro** culpam admittit, *or* **Raro** fit ut culpam admittat

After 'it is better,' *for* is rendered by the Infinitive.

* *Richard II.* ii. 2. 123.

It is better FOR *one man to suffer than* FOR *a whole nation to perish*	Melius est **civem** unum aliquid incommodi **accipere** quam **civitatem totam perire**

For often connects two nouns in the sense of **about**, as in 'a signal *for* battle,' 'grief *for* his daughter,' 'no room *for* friendship.' In this sense it is often expressed by the Latin Objective Genitive. (See Par. 33.)

For in the sense of *about* often follows English Verbs signifying desire, e.g. *to ask, long, seek, pine, search, for*. These would be rendered by single verbs in Latin, **rogo, cupio, quæro,** &c.

From (*fro-m*, where *m* is a superlative suffix; cognate with Eng. *fore*) : (1) *away from*, **a** ; (2) *down from*, **de** ; (3) *out of*, **e** ; (4) after Verb of motion, often rendered by Latin Dative, the *motion from* being expressed by the Verb of motion.

FROM *his childhood, youth, &c.*	Inde **a** parvo, **ab** adolescentia, &c.
FROM *the time when I returned*	**Ex** quo tempore redii
FROM *a slave, you became a freedman*	**E** servo libertus factus es
FROM *his name the city was called Rome*	**Ex** or **de** ejus nomine urbs Roma est nominata
I am different FROM *you*	Alius sum **ac** tu, *i.e. I am different* AND *you (are different)*
I am different FROM *what I once was*	Alius sum **atque** olim fui
He came FROM *Carthage*	**Carthagine** venit (Par. 16)
He wrested my kingdom FROM *me*	Regnum **mihi** eripuit

From (like *for*) often follows a Noun or Adjective signifying *freedom from*. In this sense *from* is often rendered by the Latin Objective Genitive, *e.g.* 'rest *from* cares,' 'requies **curarum**.' (See Par. 33.)

In, generally rendered by Latin **in**. **In** is omitted before **loco, modo, æstate, hieme**, which are used adverbially. When used metaphorically to describe the *manner* in which a thing is done, as '*in* haste,' it must be translated in Latin by an Adverb or by **cum**; but if the Noun is qualified by an Adjective, the Ablative is allowed without any Preposition. (See Par. 24.)

He answered { IN *haste* / IN *great haste* } { **Cum** celeritate / *or* **celeriter** / **Summa** celeritate } respondit

So **urbe, civitate, tota**; but **in urbe, in civitate**.

Late IN *the night*; *in the third watch*	Multa de nocte; de tertia vigilia (*Before the expiration of*)
Once IN *ten days*	Decimo quoque die
IN *England*; *in Herodotus*	**Apud** Anglos; **apud** Herodotum

In Anglia would not be used except literally, *i.e.* for *geographical* description.

In is very rarely used in good English for *into*, though it was so used by Shakespeare,* and it is still good English to say, 'he fell in love.' The Latins often use **in** in this sense, with a notion of *direction*. The Accusative which means *motion towards*, naturally follows **in** thus used.

This plain is ten miles IN *breadth*	Campus decem millia passuum **in** latitudinem patet (i.e. *extends in the direction of*)

---

* *Shakespearian Grammar*, Paragraph 159.

He spoke IN *this way* (*to this effect*)	**In** *or* **ad** hunc modum orationem habuit
He was put IN *prison*	**In** vincula conjectus est

Rule—'In,' when expressing direction,* is followed by the Accusative.

He did it IN (*influenced by*) *anger*	**Per** iram, *or* **iratus** hoc fecit
IN *my judgment*	**Me judice**
Where IN *the world ?*	Ubinam **gentium** ?
IN ACCORDANCE WITH (*i.e.* IN A MANNER NATURALLY SPRINGING OUT OF) *the letter, custom, opinion, &c.*	**Ex** literis, consuetudine, sententia, &c. (*More rarely* **de***, down from*)
IN ACCORDANCE WITH (*i.e.* IN A MANNER FOLLOWING, AGREEING WITH) *nature, the law, &c.*	**Secundum** naturam, legem, &c.
IN ADDITION TO *money*	**Præter** pecuniam
IN ADDITION TO THIS, *he had, &c.*	**Huc accedebat** ut haberet, &c.
IN THE CASE OF *Themistocles, skill was almost cunning*	**In** Themistocle peritia fere versutia fiebat
IN CASE OF *his death, what will you do ?*	**Si** mortuus erit, quid facies?
IN COMPARISON WITH *Balbus you are* (*excess*) *happy*	**Præ** (*beyond*) Balbo beatus es

* It is sometimes said that *in* after a Verb of motion governs the Accusative : but of course this is not strictly true; 'he was walking *in* a room' is **in cubiculo** ambulabat.'

IN COMPARISON WITH *Balbus you are (defect) miserable*	Miser es ad (*if you try to come up to*)Balbum. (*Or*, **conferre, comparare**)

In compliance with, **ex, secundum**; or turn by **obsequi, morem gerere**.

In consequence of, **ex, propter**, or turn by a Verb or Participle.

IN CONSEQUENCE OF *this defeat the consul retreated to Mutina*	**Qua clade coactus** consul Mutinam se recepit
I was going IN THE DIRECTION OF *Arpinum*	Ibam Arpinum **versus**
I am IN FAVOUR OF *you*	**A** te **sto**
This is IN FAVOUR OF *Balbus*	Hoc **a**, *or* **cum** Balbo **facit**
He wishes to abdicate IN FAVOUR OF *his son*	Vult **ita** se regno abdicare **ut succedat** filius
IN THE MIDST OF *the enemy*	**Mediis** in hostibus
He spoke IN OPPOSITION TO *the proposal*	**Contra** sententiam dicebat
This is IN OPPOSITION TO *that*	Hæc ab illis **discrepant**
IN POINT OF *numbers*	**Numero**, *or* **quod attinet ad** numerum

In presence of. (See *Before.*)

IN QUEST (or SEARCH) OF *truth we ought to grudge no labour*	Veritatem **conquirentes** dedecet labori parcere
IN RESPECT OF *natural ability and education he was no way deficient*	Nihil illi neque a natura neque a doctrina defuit
IN SPITE OF *all the citizens could do*	Civibus omnia nequicquam tentantibus

In spite of *my interces-*   Me frustra deprecante
sion

Inside of, intra. (See *Within.*)

Instead of: (1) *as a substitute for,* **pro**; (2) *as good as,* **loco** (with Gen.); (3) **in vicem** or **vice** is used in later Latin for *as a substitute for.*

Are you ready to die IN-STEAD OF *your friend?*	Num **pro** amico vis mori?
He was as it were INSTEAD OF *a brother to me*	**Loco** fratris erat mihi
Bitumen was used IN-STEAD OF *mortar*	Bitumen **vice** arenæ interstratum
INSTEAD OF *love he gives us hatred*	Odit, **quum** amare debeat. (Par. 75.)

Including, inclusive of.

There are in all two hundred of us, INCLUDING *women and children*	Omnino ducenti sumus, **si** mulieres liberosque **annumeraveris**

Like is irregularly used as a Preposition (in the same way as *near*): 'I write *like* her.' See Conjunctions, *As.*

Near: (1) **prope** with Acc.; (2) *close to,* **propter**; (3) *at,* **apud**; (4) *near, off, of land and naval battles,* **ad**; (5) *hard by,* **juxta.** Note the expression '**prope absum** ab aliquo loco' for 'I am *near* a place.'

Of (*akin* to *off,* ἀπό, **ab**); (1) *motion from;* (2) *out of;* (3) *in consequence of;* (4) *connection of any kind;* (5) *belonging to;* (6) *about.*

Ireland is on the south-west OF *Scotland*	Hibernia ab occasu æstivo **ad** Scotiam spectat

He is within a mile OF *the city*	Ab urbe minus mille passus abest
This comes OF *laziness*	Hunc habet **fructum** ignavia
He comes OF *good parentage*	**Parentibus** non humilibus **ortus est**
A cup OF *gold*	Poculum **ex** auro **factum**, *or simply* **aureum**
A man OF *Athens*	Civis **Atheniensis** (*not* **Athenarum**)
The vigour OF *youth*	Vigor **juvenum** *or* **juvenilis**
A man of ability	Vir **ingeniosus** (*not* **ingenii**)

But,

A man OF *great ability*	Vir **summi ingenii** *or* **summo ingenio**
Three hundred OF *the citizens* } *survive*	Trecenti **ex** civibus supersunt
All OF *us*	**Nos** omnes supersumus
The city OF *Rome*	Urbs **Roma**
The battle OF *Cannæ*	Prælium **ad Cannas pugnatum**, *or* **Cannense**
The top OF *the tree, mountain, &c.*	Summa **arbor**, summus **mons**, &c.
Don't stir a finger's breadth, no not a hair's breadth from this spot	Ne hinc transversum **digitum**, ne latum quide **unguem** abscesseris
After the consulship OF *Tullius*	Post **consulem Tullium**
He died (IN CONSEQUENCE) OF *hunger*	**Inedia*** periit

* Compare for the use of the Ablative:
'Which is as bad as die *with* tickling.'
Much Ado about Nothing, iii. 1. 80

News OF (ABOUT) *his death has arrived*	Fama **de** illius morte **huc** adlata est
What will become OF *my brother?*	Quid **de** fratre fiet?
What do you think OF *this?*	Quid **de** his putas?
Swift OF *foot* (A-FOOT), *ready* OF *wit*	Velox **pedibus,** alacer **animo**

Of is used partitively in English after *eat, taste;* but an Accusative follows **edere, gustare.**

Of, in the sense of *about,* **de,** is common after *inform, know, think, glad, despair, doubt.*

Off, *motion from,* **de ;** then of situation nautically, *some way from:* this the Latins render by **contra, ad, propter,** or by the **ob** in **objacet,** the Verb being followed by the Dative.

The battle took place OFF *Actium*	Pugnatum est **ad** Actium

On (connected with *in*): (1) *rest or motion on, in, or near something:* (2) metaphorically, *on or in a certain time:* (3) *position above,* **super** or* Participle ; (4) metaphorically, *resting on as a basis, in consequence of, after:* (5) metaphorically, *about,* **de ;** (6) metaphorically, as an Adverbial Prefix.

N.B.—*On* after a verb of motion is often rendered by **in** with Acc., and, after a compound Latin Verb, by a Dative. (See Par. 15.)

Did you not put him ON *the rack?*	Nonne eum **in** equuleum imposuisti?

* E.g. '*On* his shield,' 'clypeo **exceptum,** or **supposito.**

ON *earth* (*as opposed to heaven*)	**Apud** mortales; **in** hac vita. (**Terra** would mean *by land*.)
ON *the Appian road*	**In** Appia via
He has a wreath ON *his head*	Coronam **in** capite habet
London is ON *the Thames*	Londinium **ad** Tamesin situm est
ON *the north, rear, &c.*	**A** Septentrione, tergo, &c.
ON *our journey*	**Ex** itinere. (Par. 39.)
We held a conference ON *horseback*	**Ex** equis collocuti sumus
I heard her play ON (WITH THE INSTRUMENTALITY OF) *the lyre, harp, &c.*	Audivi illam **lyra, cithara,** &c. canentem
I feed ON *bread*	**Pane** vescor
ON *foot;* ON *our knees*	**Pedibus; genibus**
ON *the 26th of October*	**Ante diem septimum Kalendas Novembres**
ON *the next, tenth, &c. day*	**Postero, decimo,** &c. die
ON (IN THE FRONT PART OF) *the platform*	**Pro** suggestu
They carried him home ON *his own shield*	**Clypeo** suo (N.B. not **ejus**, as *his own* is emphatic) eum **exceptum** referebant
ON *condition that you promise*	**Ita** *or* **Ea lege** *or* **ea conditione** (*rarely* **sub ea**) ut promittas (*also* **Ita** *or* **Ea lege** si promiseris)
ON THE COMPLETION, TERMINATION OF *his consulship*	**Ex** consulatu **Consulatu peracto**
ON (ABOUT) *this point I have nothing to say*	**De** hac re nihil habeo quod dicam

Par. 41.] 'ON.' 49

E

ON *a sudden;* ON *purpose*	**Subito; consulto, de industria**
He is ON *the watch for a fault*	**Expectat** dum pecces
Evils come one ON *another*	Calamitates alia **ex** alia insequuntur. (See *After*.)
When he was ON THE POINT OF *death*	Quum **in eo** erat **ut moreretur**
I am ON *Cæsar's* SIDE	Sentio **cum, pro** Cæsare
I am ON *neither* SIDE	Neutrius **partis** sum
This is ON *our* SIDE	Hoc **a** nobis facit
ON THE SIDE OF *the Helvetii the country is shut in by mountains*	**Ab** Helvetiis montes regionem includunt
ON THIS SIDE, ON THAT SIDE, OF *the Alps*	**Cis, ultra** Alpes
He excuses himself ON THE PLEA OF *health*	Morbi **causa** sese excusat (Instrumentality)

On account of, propter; ob; after negative, **præ, per; ergo** with a Genitive after its case, archaic. Also:

It is ON ACCOUNT OF *my friends that I grieve*	Equidem amicorum **vicem** doleo

Opposite, (1) literally and metaphorically, **contra;** (2) literally, **ex adverso, exadversus,** followed by Genitive or Dative; (3) *right over against*, **e regione** followed by Genitive or Dative; (4) nautically used, *off*, rendered by **ob** in **objacet** or **oppositum.**

Out of, (1) after a Verb of motion, literally, **ex ;** (2) *outside, beyond,* **extra ;** (3) metaphorically *as a result of, on account of,* **propter, per,** or the Ablative with Participle.

OUT OF *shot*	**Extra** teli jactum
He obeys the laws OUT OF *fear*	Legibus **propter metum,** or **metu coactus** paret

He did it OUT OF *fun*	**Per** jocum id fecit
He is OUT OF *his mind*	**Minus** est sui compos
It is OUT OF *our power to acquit one who is guilty*	**Non** est ea potestas nostra ut sontem absolvamus

Outside of, extra.

Over (1), *motion or rest over*, **super**; *all over*, **per**; (2) *across*, **trans**; (3) *rest over*, **supra**; (4) metaphorically, *more than*, **super** (but better **amplius**); (5) metaphorically, *extending over*, *during*, **per**, or Accusative of duration; (6) where *over* denotes superiority in authority, it is generally represented by some compound Verb, *e.g.* **præsum** containing **præ** and governing the Dative. *Over and above* is **super** or **præter**.

We shall pass OVER *the Rhine*	**Trans** Rhenum transjiciemus (the Preposition may be omitted)
The plague lasted OVER *a period of ten years*	Pestis **decem** (or **per decem**) **annos** durabat
He was set OVER *the army*	**Exercitui** præfectus est
OVER AGAINST	**E regione** (from the direction) followed by Gen. or Dat.

Owing to. Per, propter, ob.

It was OWING TO *you that I did not succeed*	**Per te** stetit quominus res mihi prospere succederet

Pending.

PENDING *the decision of the judge, the plaintiff disappeared*	**Ante quam judicari posset,** petitor subito abierat (or **re nondum judicata**)

Previous to, ante, Prep., or **antequam, priusquam,** Conj. See *Before*, and also Paragraph 66.

Regarding (see *With regard to*).

Respecting (see *With respect to*).

Relatively to.

Our loss, though great absolutely, is yet very slight RELATIVELY TO *that of the enemy*	Cladem re ipsa magnam, sed **cum hostium clade comparatam**, levissimam accepimus

Round, Around, (1) **circum**; (2) *round about*, less exactly, **circa**. Sometimes expressed by a compound, *e.g.* **circumdare**.

He built a wall ROUND *the city*	Urbi murum **circumdedit**
We must send ambassadors ROUND TO *the neighbouring nations*	Legati **circa** vicinas gentes mittendi

Since (1) with a notion of consequence, *from,* **ex**; (2) dating back from a starting point, with notion of continuousness, **a, inde a**; (3) with negative as in 'never *since*,' **post**.

Ever SINCE *the beginning of the building of the bridge*	**Ex eo tempore** quo pons institui cœptus est. (Do not omit **eo tempore** *in prose*.)
SINCE *his childhood*	**Inde** a puero
Never SINCE *the creation of the world*	Nunquam **post** homines natos

Through (akin to **trans**, Germ. *durch*) (1) radical meaning, *motion across and out of, through the midst of,* **per**; (2) applied to time, *throughout, during,* **per**; (3) metaphorically, *indirect agency,* **per** (see *Owing to*), but also turned by **opera, beneficio**.

It was THROUGH *me that you recovered Tarentum*	**Mea opera** Tarentum recepisti
THROUGH *his wealth he rose to be king*	Divitiarum **beneficio** rex exortus est

Till (O.E. *til* = *to*), **ad; usque ad.** Often to be turned by a Conjunction in Latin. (See 66.)

To,* (1) meaning *motion to* or *into*, **ad, in**; (2) *extension of space to*, **usque ad, tenus**; (3) *extension of time to*, **ad, in**; (4) *extension of number to*, **ad**; (5) *motion to*, hence *object, purpose, result*, **in, ad**; (6) *motion to, and hence comparison with*, **ad**; (7) *relation to, conduct to*, **erga, in**; (8) loosely used for *as regards*.

He will go first TO *Athens, then* TO *Italy*	Primum Athenas ibit, tum **in** Italiam. (Par. 16.)
His kingdom extends TO *Taurus*	Tauro **tenus** regnat
They fought TO *a late hour in the day*	**In** multum diei pugnatum est
We lost TO *the number of fifty men; the enemy were killed* TO *a man*	Nostrorum **ad** quinquaginta, hostes **ad** unum occisi
TO *what end do you say this?*	Quem **ad** finem (*or* **quorsum**) hæc dicis?
This is TO *the purpose*	Hæc **in** rem sunt
He spoke TO *this effect*	**In** hanc sententiam dixit (*or* **In** hunc modum)
Though he's a good fellow, he's nothing TO *Balbus*	Homo est, ut bonus, ita nihil **ad** Balbum
He was dutiful TO *his parents, and strictly loyal* TO *his king*	Pius erat **in** parentes, perpetua **erga** regem fide

* For *to* before Verbs see Paragraph 73.

To *my mind, you are wrong*	Peccas, **me judice** Peccare **mihi quidem videris**
To *the best of his power*	**Pro** virili parte
I would TO *God I could help him*	**Ita me Dii ament,** ut velim ei subvenire

Touching: (1) *as to*, **quod attinet ad, quod ad**; (2) *concerning*, **de**.

Toward: (1) *motion in the direction of*, **adversus**; (2) *in the direction of* (sometimes without motion), **ad, in**; (3) of time, **sub** with Accusative; (4) in relation to persons, **erga, in**, with Accusative.

They charged TOWARD *the hill which looks* TOWARD *the north*	Impetum **adversus** collem fecerunt, qui **in** *or* **ad** Septentriones spectat
TOWARD *night*	**Sub** noctem
He feels TOWARD *him the love of a brother*	Amore **in** eum fraterno est

Under: literally and metaphorically **sub**; followed by Ablative, but after Verbs of motion, by Accusative.

Some metaphors, such as '*under* a pretence,' '*under* this head,' are rendered in Latin literally, and not metaphorically, *e.g.* '**per** speciem,' '**in** hoc genere,' '*by means of* a pretence,' '*in* this class.'

This is placed by Balbus UNDER *the first head, but seems to me to come* UNDER *the other*	Hoc a Balbo quidem **in primo** genere ponitur, mihi autem **in alterum** videtur venire
UNDER *pretence of friendship, and* UNDER *a show of bringing about a peace*	**Per** simulationem amicitiæ, et **per** speciem pacis reconciliandæ

UNDER *arms*	In armis
UNDER *appearance of favour*	Specie (adv.) beneficii
UNDER *your guidance*	Te duce
UNDER *this condition that, &c.*	Ea lege ut, &c.
UNDER *these circumstances*	Quæ cum ita sint

Until (see Till).

Unto (see To).

With, radical meaning 'from, against' (MORRIS): hence, from meaning 'opposite,' it comes to have the meanings of (1) *neighbourhood, relations friendly or hostile*, **cum**; (2) *in the hands of*, **penes**; (3) *circumstance*, **cum** or Abl. with Adjective; (4) *instrument*, Abl.; (5) *circumstance regarded as a cause*, '*considering*,' **pro**; (6) in adverbial phrases to signify *manner*, Latin Adverb.

WITH *whom does the decision rest?*	Penes quem est arbitrium?
He came WITH *speed*	Cum celeritate venit. (Or summa celeritate.)
WITH *heaven's aid*	Diis juvantibus
WITH *your usual wisdom, you will be on your guard*	Tu, pro tua prudentia cavebis
WITH *pleasure, reluctance*	Libenter, invitus
They fight WITH (AMONG) *one another instead of* WITH (AGAINST, OPPOSITE TO) *the enemy*	Inter sese pugnant quum debeant pugnare cum hoste
Having the wind WITH *him*	Ventum secundum nactus
WITH *all my heart*	Ex animo (*i.e.* from the bottom of my heart)

It is all over WITH *us*	Actum est de nobis
What shall we do WITH *it?*	{ Quid de hoc faciemus? Quomodo **hoc utemur**?

The Verbs *I am angry with*, **irascor (tibi)**; *I go on with*, i.e. *continue*, **persequor**; *I find fault with*, **reprehendo**; *I agree with*, **assentior (tibi)**, illustrate the fact that *with* is often a part of a Compound Transitive Verb, and is not to be rendered by a Latin Preposition.

I am the same * WITH *you*	Idem sum **ac** tu, *i.e.* I am the same *and* you are (the same)
I fear it equally WITH *you*	Hoc, æque **ac** tu, vereor
He was at Rome at the same time WITH *me*	Romæ, eodem tempore **quo** ego, vitam agebat

It would be interesting to discover why other Prepositions and other Pronouns are not combined in the following way:—

Rule—'Cum' is used as an enclitic in 'mecum,' 'tecum,' 'quocum,' 'nobiscum,' 'vobiscum,' and 'quibuscum.' †

WITH REFERENCE TO WITH REGARD TO WITH RESPECT TO	**De; quod attinet ad;**

sometimes to be expressed by emphasis, with the addition of **quidem.**

WITH REFERENCE TO *Tullius, I have no ground for asking your consideration; for the rest I should like to say a word*	**Tullium** · **(quidem)** nihil habeo cur excuses; pro ceteris velim pauca dicam

* This is hardly English, but it corresponds to 'different *from.*
† '**Tenus**' in '**hactenus,**' '**quatenus.**

With a view to (ad; in; causa with Gen.; or turn by eo consilio ut).

They all act WITH A VIEW TO *their own interests*	Omnes sibi quisque consulunt

Within: (1) of time, space, **intra**; (2) *on this side of*, **cis, citra**.

He was WITHIN A LITTLE *of death*	Minimum abfuit quin periret

Without: (1) *want* or *absence*, **sine**; (2) *outside*, **extra**; (3) turn by Participle, Conjunction, or Adverb.

He was condemned WITHOUT *a hearing*	Inauditus damnatus est
'*Strong* WITHOUT *rage*'	{ Valet, neque tamen furit { Ita valet ut non furat
He acted WITHOUT *discretion*	Imprudenter fecit

42. Ellipse of English Prepositions. The Preposition *by* is expressed in English to denote the measure of excess or defect, *e.g.* 'shorter, taller *by* five feet.' But when the amount of excess or defect is mentioned *before* the Comparative, the Preposition is omitted, '(*by*) five feet taller,' where 'five feet' is used, like 'this side,' adverbially. The Latins make no difference whether the Comparative precede or follow.

(BY) *so much the better*	Eo melius
(BY) *how far he surpasses!*	Quanto superat!
MUCH WORSE	Multo pejus
He's (BY) *a little too late*	Paullo est tardior

Rule—The measure of excess or defect is expressed by the Ablative, *e.g.* 'quinque pedibus major.'

Some prepositional phrase, e.g. *to the extent of, amount of*, seems to be required before *high, deep, broad*, &c. The Latins express this absent Preposition mostly by the Accusative case, 'Agger erat decem **pedes** altus;' or else, less frequently, by the Accusative after **habebat**, *e.g.* 'decem pedes **habebat altus**.'

43. Conjunctions, Coordinate and Subordinate. Coordinate Conjunctions are those that conjoin sentences that are parallel and not subordinate the one to the other. Thus in 'I came *and, but, so, therefore*, he returned,' we have two coordinate sentences connected by *and*, &c. But in 'I came *because* he returned,' *I came* is the statement or principal sentence, and *he returned* is only introduced as a reason, *i.e.* subordinately. This may be illustrated by a diagram.

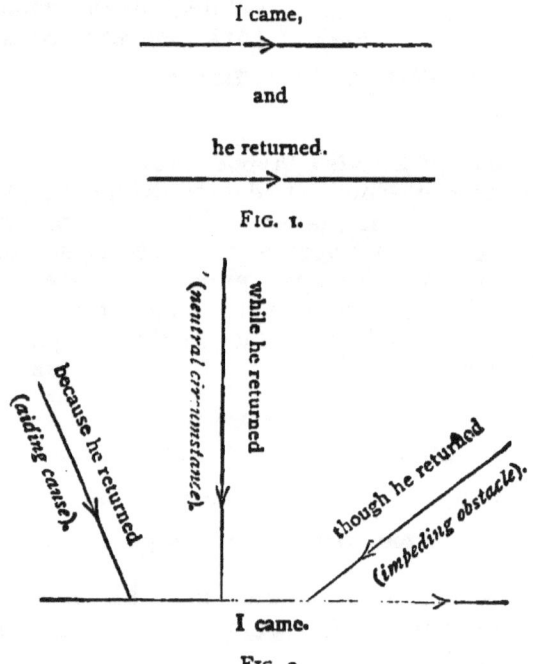

FIG. 1.

FIG 2.

In the first diagram the two sentences are parallel; in the second diagram, the sentence *he returned* is (1) an aiding cause, or (2) a neutral circumstance, or (3) an impeding obstacle, and, in each of the three cases, *Subordinate*.

44. Conjunctions Co-ordinate. *And* is added in English, illogically but usefully, to prepare the hearer for the last of a number of things enumerated, 'John, Thomas, *and* (*lastly*) Harry.' The Latins, not disliking the abruptness, or preferring logical symmetry to smoothness, say, 'Johannes, Thomas, Henricus,' or 'Johannes et Thomas et Henricus.'

Rule—In enumerations, ' et ' must be used throughout or not at all.

44a. Enclitic Conjunctions. *Too* (meaning *also*), e.g. 'You *too*, Brutus!' must follow some emphatic word and cannot stand first in a sentence. The Latins have many such Enclitic Conjunctions.

Rule—'Autem,' 'enim,' 'quidem,' 'que,' 've,' 'vero,'* and generally 'igitur' and 'tamen,' cannot stand first in a sentence, but must follow some emphatic word.

N.B.—Distinguish between **sed** and **autem**. **Sed** (se-d *by itself*, something *distinct* from what precedes) qualifies, corrects, or denies : **autem** *whereas, while* (Greek δι), introduces a second statement not inconsistent with the first. Distinguish also between **verum** *but*, and **vero** *truly*.

| *He is a little dull;* WHILE *you are clever*, BUT *unstable in all your actions* | Ille quidem tardior ; tu autem ingeniosus, **sed** in omni vita inconstans |

* **Vero** stands first in replies, *e.g.* 'Will you come? Yes, and gladly.' '**Vero**, ac libenter quidem.'

But introducing an objection abruptly is to be rendered **at enim**.

BUT *you were compelled to do it*, YOU SAY   **At enim** vi coactus fecisti

45. Negative Conjunctions. In English we do not shrink from saying 'and not,' 'and no one;' but *and* means +, while *not* often means —, and the Latins felt the impropriety of saying '**et non**' '+, —,' where the positive and negative are equally emphatic. They preferred to *bring the negative to the front*, and had at command the unemphatic form of *and*, **que**. They therefore preferred to say **neque**, and also **nec quisquam**. So **neve, nisi**. For a similar reason the Latins dislike **non valde**, and prefer **non ita**. They also prefer **nego** to 'dico .... non.'

Rule—' And not,' ' and no one,' ' if not,' are to be rendered by ' neque,' ' nec quisquam,' ' nisi.' So also ' neque unquam,' ' usquam,' &c.

We say 'not even Balbus:' but, in Latin, **quidem**, being an enclitic (44a.) must come after the word that it qualifies. Note therefore the following:—

Rule—Do not say ' ne quidem Balbus,' but ' ne Balbus quidem.'

46. ' And he,' ' now he.' The Latins, greatly disliking **ille** and **is** to represent a previous Subject, prefer **qui**, to denote the Subject *with the notion of connection*.

Rule—' And he,' ' now he,' &c. must often be rendered by ' qui.'

I called on the man AND HE *told me*, &c.   Conveni hominem, **qui** me certiorem fecit, &c.

Now *since* THIS *is so*	**Quæ** quum ita sint
Now *when he heard* THIS ..	**Quibus** auditis ...

He also is often **idem.**

Epicurus denied this : HE ALSO *maintained that pain is the greatest possible evil*	Epicurus hoc negabat. **Idem** dictitabat summum malum esse dolorem

47. 'And' and 'but' omitted. The Latins dislike a long string of coordinate clauses, and avoid them by using sometimes Participles, sometimes Conjunctions. In English the power of converting almost any Participle into an Adjective, *e.g.* 'the *burned* cake,' prevents us from using the Participle in the same way in which the Latins use it. We could not say 'he left the *burned* bridge' for 'he *burned and* left the bridge.' The Latins greatly prefer the Participial construction.

Rule—'He burned and left the bridge' = 'Pontem incensum deseruit.'

But is also sometimes omitted in the same way:

I asked him what he wanted, BUT *he made no reply*	**Interroganti** mihi quid vellet nihil respondit

'*But,*' '*while,*' should be omitted where two statements, or questions implying statements, are combined for the purpose of bringing out the absurdity of the combination. The Latins are fond of occasional abruptness.

How! are we to suppose that this is possible for boys, BUT *impossible for men?*	Quid igitur! Hoc pueri possunt, viri non possunt?

But used for *that not*, see Paragraph 55.

48. Subordinate Conjunctions. We will first consider those that introduce a Subjective or Objective clause.

That. Take the sentence 'he is honest.' If this is to be made the Object of a Transitive Verb, *e.g.* 'I know,' we can say 'I know *him to be honest*,' where the Object of *know* is not *him*, but *him to be honest*. So the Latins say 'certo scio **illum probum esse**.' But, whether it be that we dislike the juxtaposition of the Transitive Verb, e.g. *know*, with a Pronoun, e.g. *him*, that is not really the Object of that Verb, or whatever be the reason, we cannot use this construction in many cases. For example, we cannot *now* say 'I hear or read *him to be honest*,' nor can we say 'it is certain *him to be honest*.' The Latins, more consistently, use this construction wherever a clause is introduced either as Subject or Object. 'Audio (Obj.) **illum probum esse**,' 'Certum est (Subj.) **illum probum esse**.'

In such cases we generally connect the Subject or Object with the principal Verb by *that* (*how that*) : 'I hear (Object) (*how*) *that* he is honest.' Compare in Greek λέγω ὅτι, in Low Latin 'dico **quod**,' in French 'je dis **que**.' So, '*that* he is honest (Subject) is certain.'

Rule—Do not translate 'that' by 'ut' where it introduces an Objective or Subjective Clause, but by the Infinitive, *e.g.* 'I am persuaded (I know) *that* it is true.' 'Persuasum est mihi **hæc vera esse**.'

<small>In order to prepare the way for the Object sentence, the Latins often insert an Object pronoun, or an Adverb before the Accusative and Infinitive, '**Sic** a majoribus accepimus, injurias non ferendas esse.' 'Quum sibi **ita** persuasisset ipse, &c.' Sometimes **ita** is followed by **ut** with the Subjunctive. '**Ita** a patribus didicimus **ut** virtute magis quam dolo contendamus.'</small>

N.B.—When the Infinitive has a Subject and also an Object, both in the Accusative, great care is necessary to avoid ambiguity. Thus, what is the meaning of—

'Aio te, Æacida, **Romanos** vincere posse'?

The meaning would be clear if the oracle had said 'Aio,

Pyrrhe, te a Romanis vinci posse,' using the *Passive*, instead of the Active.

Rule—Avoid the Ambiguity arising from the Accusative before and after the Infinitive.

49. Exceptions—With 'it seems *that*,' 'it is said *that*,' the Latins use the Nominative and Infinitive.

It seems that Balbus has departed	Videtur **Balbus** abiisse. (*Balbus seems, &c.*)
It is said that Balbus lived to be an old man	Fertur (dicitur) **Balbus** usque ad senectutem vixisse

Quin is **qui ne**, *by which not.* The Latins regarding doubt as *preventive*, say, instead of 'there is no doubt *that* this is true,' 'There is no doubt *by which* this should *not* be true,' 'Haud dubium est **quin** hæc vera sint,' where **quin** is **qui-ne**, *by which not.* Hence:

Rule—'That' after 'there is no doubt,' is rendered by 'quin' in Latin.

A similar kind of construction is common in Elizabethan English: 'I doubt not *but* to ride as fast as he,' *i.e.* 'I have no doubt (fear) about being *prevented* from riding.'—*Shakespearian Grammar*, Paragraph 122.

N.B.—Note the Periphrasis necessary to express a Future passive after **quin**.

There's no doubt that Europe will soon be divided into more parts	Haud dubium est quin **futurum sit** ut Europa mox in plures partes **distribuatur**

That is used in English after *I fear*, as after *I hope, think, &c.* to precede the Object of fear; 'I fear (What?) *that he will come.*' The Latins render *I fear* by **vereor**, *I watch anxiously*, which contains a notion of *purpose*.

Consequently **vereor** is followed by **ne** and the Subjunctive.

I am afraid THAT *he will come*   Vereor **ne*** veniat, i.e. *I am anxiously taking measures that he may not come*

I was afraid THAT *he would not come*   Veritus sum **ut*** veniret, i.e. *I was taking measures that he might come*

Rule—'That' after 'I fear' is rendered by 'ne,' and 'that not' by 'ut'; in both cases followed by the Subjunctive.

50. **That** is often omitted, *e.g.* 'I see (*that*) you understand.' 'I told him (*that*) it was so.' The beginner must be very careful to detect such omissions and to represent the Objective Clause by the Accusative and Infinitive.

N.B.—Distinguish most carefully the above cases of omitted *that* from the following, 'I heard you sing.' No doubt this sentence might occasionally be used for 'I heard (*that*) you sing,' *e.g.* 'I heard, from my brother, you sing better than ever': but, as a rule, it would mean 'I heard you *singing*.' The ambiguity arises from the fact that *you* has no inflection (to distinguish Nom. 'that *you* sing' from Acc. 'I heard *you* singing'), and from the loss of the Old Eng. Inf. Inflection *-en*. As the Acc. and Inf. are used to represent *that*, the Latin rule is :—

Rule—Translate 'I heard her *sing*' by 'audivi illam canentem.'

Note the greater richness of English in:

I hear THAT SHE SINGS = Audio illam **canere**

I HEARD HER { SING / (IN THE ACT OF) / SINGING } = Audivi illam **canentem**

---

* See Sequence of Tenses, 64.

51. 'Whether,' and 'if,' when introducing an Objective or Subjective clause, 'He asked *whether*, or *if, this was true,*' are rendered by (1) **utrum**, followed by **an** or **ne**, (2) **num**, in both cases followed by the Subjunctive.

N.B. Distinguish between *whether* thus introducing a dependent clause, and *whether* used to express a condition, **sive**.

He asked WHETHER *this was true or not*	Rogavit **utrum** hæc vera essent * annon
WHETHER *this is true or false, I am not troubled by it*	Hæc, **sive** vera sunt **seu** falsa, nullo modo me movent .

52. The Relative Pronoun is often equivalent to a Demonstrative Pronoun combined with some Conjunction either Coordinate or Subordinate. Sometimes, as will be seen below, it introduces a coordinate, sometimes a subordinate clause. The English Relative, whether expressed by *who* or *that*, is rendered by **qui**. In English the distinction between *who* and *that* is as follows : *Who* introduces a new fact about, while *that* introduces something essential to the complete meaning of, the antecedent. 'They succeeded in capturing the soldiers (*not all, but only those*) *that* were wounded, and also the children, *who* (*for they*) were left behind as an encumbrance.'

Now, wherever *who* introduces simply a new fact, without any notion of *cause, purpose, obstacle, &c.*, and wherever *that* introduces simply something essential to the completion of the Antecedent, without any notion of *such a kind that*, the Latins, like ourselves, use the Relative with the Indicative. But in the exceptional cases above mentioned, where not a *fact* merely but a *thought* is introduced, the Latins, whose language is richer than ours in Moods, use the Subjunctive Mood to express the *thought*, as distinguished from the *fact*, the *fact* being expressed by the Indicative.

* See Sequence of Tenses, 64

THE RELATIVE PRONOUN. [Par. 52.

Rule—Wherever the Relative introduces a thought, and not merely a fact, it is followed by the Latin Subjunctive.

Some THAT *had heard it from his own lips brought me word of it*	**Qui** ex ipso **audivissent** certiorem me fecerunt

Here the Subjunctive denotes not a simple *fact*, but a *thought*, that the evidence of the class of witnesses here described is peculiarly convincing.

Rule — Since classification implies 'a thought,' the Subjunctive follows 'sunt, erant, qui,' 'there are some (such) that.'

There are some THAT *say this is not true*	Sunt **qui negent** hæc vera esse (*so sceptical that*)
Caius Ligarius doth bear Cæsar hard, WHO* (BECAUSE HE) *rated him for speaking well of Pompey*	Caius Ligarius succenset Cæsari **qui** se **culpaverit** quod Pompeium laudaverit (*so critical that*)
Balbus is one THAT (SUCH THAT) *has always consulted the interests of his country rather than his own*	Balbus is est **qui** semper reipublicæ potius quam sibi **consuluerit** (*so patriotic that*)
As for you, WHO (SINCE YOU) *have not slept for three nights, you are indeed to be pitied*	Tu quidem miserrimus, **qui** tertiam jam noctem non **dormieris** (*so much troubled that*)

* Not a common use in modern English. See *Shakespearian Grammar* Paragraph 263.

There is not a soldier, WHO (provided that he) is also a man, THAT would not recoil with horror from such a plan	Miles est nemo, **qui** modo **sit** homo, **qui*** **non** hæc perhorrescat (*so hard-hearted that*)

Qui takes the Subjunctive, even when introducing a mere defining sentence, if that sentence is a part of *a statement or opinion of some one distinct from the writer.* This is a distinction that cannot be tersely expressed in English:

Socrates used to execrate the man THAT *was the first to separate (as Socrates said) expediency from right*	Socrates exsecrari eum solebat, **qui** primus utilitatem a jure **sejunxisset**

Qui also takes the Subjunctive, where the previous construction is such as to convey the notion that the Relative Clause does not introduce *a fact i.e.* **in Subordinate Propositions dependent on clauses containing Infinitives or Subjunctives.** The following are examples:

It is natural for power to be arbitrary (do WHAT *it likes)*	Potentis est **facere quod velit**
It is easy for you to advise me to keep myself in health SO FAR AS *I can*	Facile me admones ut me salvum, **quoad possim, servem**

53. The Dependent Interrogative. *What* requires care. Where it means *that which*, it is to be rendered by **quod** or **id quod**, e.g. '*What* you say is true,' '**Quod** dicis, verum est.' But interrogatively, *what?* is rendered by **quid**? '**quid dicis?**' And the Latins, with their habitual distinction between *fact* and *not fact*, not only change **quod** into **quid**, but also change the Indicative into a Subjunctive, in a dependent Interrogative:

---

* When **nemo** is at some distance from the Relative, **quin** is sometimes replaced by **qui non**. See Paragraph 55.

Rule—In dependent interrogatives, *e.g.* 'I ask *what* you say,' 'quid' must be used, and the Verb must be in the Subjunctive, *e.g.* 'Rogo quid dicas.'

The Latins in many cases prefer the Dependent Interrogative form to the ordinary Relative.

I perceived the great kindness with WHICH *I was received by my host*	Intellexi **quanta** benevolentia hospes me **exciperet**
Do you forget the many victories THAT *you have gained?*	Num obliviscimini **quot** victorias **reportaveritis ?**

N.B.—Do not make the mistake of writing **victoriarum**, as though the Noun were governed by **obliviscor**. The Object of **obliviscor** is, not **victorias**, but *the whole of the following sentence.*

Very often *the*, qualifying the Antecedent, implies *great*, *e.g.* 'I perceived *the* kindness with which.' In all such cases **quantus** should be used. See Paragraph 21.

Rule—When 'the,' qualifying an Antecedent, implies 'great' or 'many,' 'quantus' or 'quot' should be used instead of the Relative, and should be followed by the Subjunctive.

54. 'That' after Superlatives. The English often use a Superlative preceded by *the* before the Relative : thus 'He sent me *the most beautiful* flowers (of the flowers) *that* he had.' But in Latin, 'Misit ad me pulcerrimos flores quos habuit' might mean 'He sent me some very beautiful flowers that he had.' To avoid this, the Latins place the Superlative in the Relative clause, 'Whatever (flowers) he had most beautiful, those flowers he sent,' 'Quos flores habuit pulcerrimos, eos ad me misit,' or

'Misit ad me flores, quos habuit pulcerrimos.' *All* is transposed in the same way:

All THAT *were captured were put to death*	**Qui** capti sunt, ii **omnes** interfecti
The men THAT *were in the ship*	**Ii qui** / **Si qui** / **Qui** } in navi erant.

Not **homines qui**, which might mean *some men, who*.

There are other ways of rendering *all . . . that*:

They will give up ALL *the wealth* THAT *they have remaining*	**Quidquid** / **Si quid** } divitiarum superest, id **omne** tradent

Note cases where the Relative is implied in English, *e.g.* 'The vigour of youth,' by itself, may be rendered **vigor juvenilis;** but

I have lost ALL THE *vigour of youth*	**Quem** quondam juvenis vigorem habui, **eum omnem** perdidi

Rule—Transpose the Relative in 'the best that,' 'all that,' 'the men that.'

N.B.—The Relative where used with the Indicative to *define*, often precedes its Antecedent. This may be a trace of its interrogative origin. (*Shakesp. Gram.* Par. 251.)

55. 'That . . . not,' 'but.' When *that* has for its Antecedent *no one* or *nothing*, and is followed by *not, that not* are often combined in Latin and rendered by **quin (qui-ne)**.

There was NO ONE THAT *did* NOT *weep*	Nemo erat **quin** fleret

When *that* is the Object of a Verb, '**quem . . . . non**' is preferable to '**quin . . . . eum.**'

There was no one THAT *Tullius did* NOT *love*	Nemo erat **quem** Tullius **non** amaret

N.B.--*But* meaning *except* is often used for 'that . . . not.' 'There was no one *but* wept,' *i.e.* strictly, 'there was no one *except* those that wept.' *But* seems loosely used as a negative Relative, just as *as* is used as a positive Relative in 'Such flowers *as** I have, I will give.' In Latin, *but* is rendered by **quin** or **qui . . . non**.

| *There is no one* BUT *hates me* | Nemo est **quin** me oderit |

56. 'That' after repeated Antecedent. When the English Antecedent is repeated, or stands, loosely, in apposition to a previous sentence, it is attracted, in Latin, into the Relative clause:

| *He answered me with the greatest courtesy —* A COURTESY THAT *I shall never forget* | Summa comitate mihi respondit: **cujus comitatis** equidem nunquam obliviscar |
| *He lightened the taxes,* A KINDNESS THAT *secured him the favour of his countrymen* | Vectigalium onera levabat: **quo beneficio** cives conciliabat |

N.B.—You may turn sentences of this kind in some other way: but you must *never render them literally*.

57. 'That' for 'when.' *That*, after an Antecedent of Time, is used for 'on that,' *i.e.* 'on which,' and is therefore equivalent to *when*.

| *On the day* THAT (ON WHICH, WHEN) *thou eatest thereof* | **Quo die** hoc gustaveris |

When a Negative precedes *that* thus used, the Relative and Negative are often combined and rendered by **quin** (**qui**, old Abl.; **ne**):

---

* Shakespeare writes sometimes 'such *which*.' See page 72, note.

| *Not a day passes* THAT *he does not come here* | Dies fere nullus **quin huc** ventitet |

58. Omission of the Relative. The Relative is often omitted in English, when it would come as an Object, just between the Antecedent and a following Subject, *e.g.* 'A man (that) I saw yesterday said, &c.' The pupils must remember that the Relative is *never omitted in Latin* either in such a sentence as the above, or *with Participles*, as in the following:—

| *The soldiers* (THAT WERE) SHUT UP *in the castle* conspired *with those* (THAT WERE) REMAINING *outside the town* | **Quidquid** militum in castello clausum erat, cum iis conjurabat militibus **qui** extra oppidum manebant |

Milites clausi might mean '*the soldiers,* or *some soldiers, being shut up:*' '**iis manentibus**' would mean '*them, while remaining,*' or '*those mentioned, who* were *remaining.*'

59. Relatival Conjunctions. As (*in the way, degree in which*), **quam**: sometimes demonstrative, *in that degree,* **tam.***

| *Balbus is* AS (IN THAT DEGREE) *wise* AS (IN WHICH DEGREE) *I am* | Balbus est **tam** sapiens **quam** ego |

Sentences like these might be turned by 'equally,' *e.g.* 'Balbus and I are equally grieved,' or, less logically, 'Balbus is equally grieved and I (am equally grieved).' 'Balbus æque dolet atque ego.'

---

* In '*as* good *as*' the first *as* = *so*. In Elizabethan English *so* ... *as* was often used where we use *as* ... *as*.
'*So* well thy words become thee *as* thy wounds.'
Macbeth, i. 2. 43.

This similarity between **Demonstratives** and **Relatives** is illustrated by the double use of *that*.

You ought to have respected him AS (*you ought to have respected*) *a father*	Illum **æque** (colere debuisti) **ac** patrem colere debuisti
This is the same thing AS *asking a question of a deaf man*	Hoc est idem **ac** (idem sit) si surdum interroges (i.e. *and it would be the same*)

As (*in the way in which*) is also rendered by **ut** with the Indicative, or by **eodem modo quo**.

AS *you sow, so you must reap*	**Ut** seres, ita metes
AS *you please*	**Ut** libet
I shall answer AS *you did*	Ego respondebo **eodem modo quo** tu respondisti

As in English is sometimes used as a Subject or Object, like the Relative Pronoun, *e.g.* in the two next examples:

He said the same AS *before*	**Eadem quæ** antea, dixit
Such help AS* *I can give you I will*	**Quod** auxilium potero dare, dabo
(BEING, *or* THOUGH I AM†) *Old* AS *I am I will resist*	**Quamvis** (*to whatever degree*) senex, resistam

60. 'As,' 'like,' superlative notion of. *As* and *like* are often used, without any notion of *comparison*, to give a *Superlative* meaning, just as little boys say, 'I have *such* a beautiful toy.' The Latins, more logically, express this Superlative notion by a Superlative Adjective, or, if the meaning is clear without it, they sometimes omit the Superlative:

Who could disbelieve a man LIKE *Cato?*	Quis Catoni, **viro sanctissimo**, fidem non tribuat?

---

* 'Such I will have *whom* I am sure he knows not.'
        All's Well that Ends Well, iii. 6. 14.

† '*As* near the dawning, provost, *as* it is.'
        Measure for Measure, iv. 2. 97.

It would be monstrous that such men AS *the Gracchi should complain of unconstitutional conduct!*	Quis Gracchos, de seditione querentes, tulerit?
A man LIKE *you will always spare the conquered*	Tu, **cujus es misericordiæ,** semper victis parces
We must not desert such a brave fellow AS *Richard*	Ricardus, **vir fortissimus,** nullo modo est deserendus

Rule—'Such . . . as,' 'a man like,' must often be rendered by the Latin Superlative.

61. 'Than' expressed by 'quam.' 'Tullius is wiser *than* I,' is to be explained as follows: *Than* is a form of *the*, the old Relative, meaning *in what way*, so that the above sentence means '*In what way (whereas)* I am wise, Tullius is wiser.' So, 'In *what* way *(whereas)* you helped me, you helped no one more.' The Latin equivalent for *in what way* is **quam.** Hence:

You helped no one more THAN *me*	Nemini plus **quam** mihi subvenisti
His gift was greater in appearance THAN *in reality*	Donum dedit specie **quam** re majus

Rule—When two words are connected in the way of comparison by 'quam,' and when the Verb is the same in each member of the sentence of Comparison, the two words stand in the same case.

62. 'Than' expressed by the Ablative. Comparison may be differently expressed. 'Tallness' is relative; a man that is not 'tall' (as compared with average men) may be made to appear 'taller' *by the presence of*

Balbus. Hence Balbus may be considered as the *instrument* that makes Tullius 'tall'; and the sentence may be expressed, 'Tullius is made taller *by Balbus,*' 'Tullius procerior est **Balbo.**' But the construction is liable to ambiguity, when the first member of the comparison is expressed by a Noun that is not in the Nominative or Accusative, *e.g.* 'Donum dedit **specie majus re,**' *i.e.* 'greater *than a thing,*' or, 'greater *than in reality.*' Hence :

Rule—'Quam' cannot be replaced by the Ablative of the second member of the comparison unless the first member of the comparison is in the Nominative or Accusative.

63. 'Than,' followed by a new Verb. If the second Noun is connected with a different Verb from the first, the new Verb is generally inserted, and the second Noun put in the necessary case.

| *Such conduct would have pleased a wiser man* THAN *Balbus was then* | Talia sapientiori placuissent homini **quam** tunc erat **Balbus** |

When the first Noun is in the Accusative, the new Verb is sometimes omitted, and the second Noun is attracted into the same case as the first, *e.g.* 'Ego hominem callidiorem vidi neminem **quam Balbum.**'

If the *instrumental* force of the Ablative is kept in mind, the reason for the following caution will be evident :

N.B.—**Take care not to use the Ablative instead of 'quam' where the Adjective does not qualify either member of the comparison,** *e.g.* 'He has a taller horse than I.' Here '*I*' cannot be regarded as the *instrument* of comparison; it is not '*I,*' but 'my horse' that makes his horse appear taller. Hence :

| *He has a taller horse than* | I / MINE | Equum habet altiorem { (1) **quam ego** (habeo) { (2) **meo** |

SEQUENCE OF TENSES.

'*More than a hundred*' might be rendered by '*a hundred and more.*' This construction is common in Latin, and in it the comparison does not affect the case of the Numeral Adjective. **Plus** in **plusquam** (as well as **amplius**) is thus adverbially used.

MORE THAN *two hundred were captured*	**Ducenti** (et) **amplius** capti sunt
I see the names of MORE THAN *five hundred of my countrymen*	Nomina video **plus quam quingentorum civium**

64. Sequence of Tenses. Before entering on the other Subordinate Conjunctions, it will be well to explain the rule that will regulate the Tenses following these Conjunctions. In subordinate sentences the Tense of the subordinate Latin Verb is dependent on the Tense of the principal Verb, *e.g.*:

I ⎰ *am making*
⎱ *make*
⎰ *have made*
⎱ *have* been making*
⎰ *shall, will be making*
⎱ *shall, will make*
⎰ *shall have made*

Rogo
Rogavi
Rogabo
Rogavero

ut illi

a request that HE MAY BE PARDONED — **ignoscatur**

I ⎰ *was making*
⎱ *made*
⎰ *had made*
⎱ *had* been making*

a request

Rogabam
Rogavi
Rogaveram

ut illi

that he MIGHT BE PARDONED — **ignosceretur**

So far, the Rule in Latin is evident. **Like follows Like.** The Future and Present Tenses (for **rogavi**, when meaning 'I *have* asked,' means 'I *have* something asked,' and is therefore a Complete Present Tense) are followed by

* See Paragraph 11.

the Present Subjunctive, and the Past Tenses by the Past Subjunctive. Of course, in an English dependent sentence, *e.g.* in a sentence following 'I ask whether,' we use, according to the sense, *is*, *was*, or *has been*. But now note the Latin equivalent :

I { *am asking* / *ask* / *have asked* / *have been asking* / *shall be asking* / *shall ask* / *shall have asked* } { **Rogo** / **Rogavi** / **Rogabo** / **Rogavero** } } utrum

whether he { *is present* / *was present* / *has been present* } **adsit** / **adfuerit** N.B.

I { *was asking* / *asked* / *had asked* / *had been asking* } { **Rogabam** / **Rogavi** / **Rogaveram** } } utrum

whether he { *is present (now)* / *was present (yesterday)* / *had been present* } **adesset** / **adfuisset**

N.B.—Note that above, 'whether he *was present*' and 'whether he *has been present*,' are both expressed in Latin by 'utrum **adfuerit**.' This is a necessary and inconvenient consequence of the Latin Law of Sequence, which is so strict that it sometimes produces great ambiguity. Thus :

I have asked whether he   Rogavi utrum **venerit**
  CAME

Here it is impossible to tell from the Latin, whether *he came*, or *he has come*, is the correct translation. But the Latins cannot help this. If they had written **veniret** above, 'rogavi utrum **veniret**,' then, since **rogavi** means both *I asked* and *I have asked*, we should naturally render the sentence, not '*I have* asked whether he came,' but '*I asked* whether he came.' This is a serious deficiency arising from the poverty of the Latin language in respect of *Tenses:* for they have nothing but **rogavi** to render our two tenses, *asked* and *have asked.*

I will ask why he CAME   Interrogabo cur **venerit**
Don't you know the esteem in   Nescisne quanto in honore
  which HE WAS HELD?   **fuerit?**

Apparent exception to Sequence of Tenses. In a conditional sentence 'if I had come, what would you have done?' the Pluperfect Subjunctive is used in both cases; and, even when the sentence depends upon a Present Tense 'I know,' the Pluperfect in the Protasis 'si **venissem**' is retained. For the Tense depends upon the nature of the condition, and not on the tense of the Principal Verb. But the Pluperfect in the Apodosis is changed, according to the Rule of Sequence, 'Scio quid **facturus fueris** si venissem,' 'I know what you would have done, if I had come,' where the condition is expressed by the Future Participle.

65. Subordinate Conjunctions. (1) time: *after (that), before (that), now that, since, until, when, while;* (2) circumstance: *whereas, while;* (3) reason: *as, in that, because, inasmuch as, seeing that;* (4) condition: *if, provided that, supposing, whether, although, however, unless;* (5) result: *so as, so that, in such a way, manner, &c. that;* (6) purpose: *in order that, so that, to the intent that, lest.*

The above list includes only those of the Prepositional Conjunctions that are followed by a Subject and a Tense of the Verb, e.g. '*before* he came.' But practically many other Prepositions are Conjunctions though only used with Verbals or (in the case of *to*) with an Infinitive: (1) circumstance: *besides, instead of, without;* (2) instrument: *by, of;* (3) reason, cause: *for, on;* (4) condition, *in spite of;* (5) purpose: *to, from.*

66. Time. It will be seen that the Latins are forced to supply their weakness in Prepositional and other Conjunctions, and also in Verbals, by using their strength in Moods. In this way the same Conjunction, *e.g.* **quum,** may be used, (1) to denote *time* with the Indicative, (2) to denote *thought* (whether it be (1) *cause*, 'since,' or (2) *succession*, with notion of consequence 'upon,' or (3) *contrast*, 'though,' 'whereas') with the Subjunctive.

SINCE *this is so, what in the world will you do?*	Quæ **quum** ita **sint**, quidnam facies?
WHEN *I used to live at Athens, I used to attend Balbus' lectures*	**Quum** Athenis **agebam**, Balbum audiebam

N.B.—In narrating the *past*, when we mention one event as occurring simultaneously with the occurrence or completion of another event, we generally imply some further connection than *at the time when*, e.g. '*when* he heard this, he fled.' Here there is a *thought*, viz. that the flight was a *consequence* of hearing. Such a sentence would be rendered in Latin 'Quæ quum **audivisset**.'

Rule—'Quum' with the Imperfect and Pluperfect generally takes the Subjunctive.

After (that), postquam. In English when we use *after* for *when*, we generally desire to express that the first action is *completed* before the second begins, e.g. '*when* he *heard* me,' but '*after* he *had heard* me.' The Latins, on the contrary, generally use, in this sense, the Pluperf. Subj. with **quum**, and the Perf. Ind. with **postquam**.

Rule—'Postquam' takes the Perfect, unless the interval is expressed or emphatically implied.

AFTER *the rebellion* HAD BEEN PUT DOWN *he returned to Rome*	**Postquam** seditio **compressa est** Romam rediit
Ten years AFTER *the rebellion* HAD BEEN *put down, he &c.*	**Decimo anno** postquam seditio **compressa erat**, &c.

As (1) **postquam** is generally used of time without expressing *thought*, it is followed by the Indicative. Else, use

(2) **quum** with Subjunctive, or (3) the Ablative Absolute,* '**seditione compressa**,' or (4) **post** governing a Noun qualified by a Participle or by some word used as a Participle, '**post seditionem compressam**,' '**post Tullium consulem**.'

Before (that), antequam, priusquam, donec (like **postquam**) take the Perfect where we often use the Pluperfect. But they differ from **postquam** in that they are often used with the Subjunctive to imply 'thought' as well as sequence.

Rule—'**Antequam**,' '**priusquam**,' '**dum**,' '**donec**,' and '**quoad**,' are followed by the Subjunctive when design is implied, or when an action is referred to that has not actually commenced.

They retired (on purpose) BEFORE *the city was (could be) captured*	**Ante** sese receperunt **quam** urbs **caperetur**

Note also the logical use of the Future in Latin (see Paragraph 11):

BEFORE *I see you*	**Antequam** te **videbo** *or* **videro**

Before is sometimes expressed by an Ablative Absolute with **nondum**, *e.g.* '**nondum** urbe condita,' or by **ante** governing a Noun qualified by a Participle, '**ante urbem conditam**.' The following sentences illustrate the Latin rendering of English Conjunctions of time:—

NOW THAT *he had arrived at Rome the young man felt sure of success*	Tum vero adolescens, **quum** Romam **venisset**, omnia spe præsumebat (Notion of *cause*)

---

* The Ablative, denoting some *circumstance*, something *with* which an action takes place, seems naturally used in this way.

SINCE *we began our journey we have not seen a man*	**Ex quo** tempore profecti sumus ne unum quidem hominem vidimus
SINCE *we began our journey we have seen two hundred men*	**Postquam** profecti sumus, homines ducentos vidimus
UNTIL *I* (FACT) *came to Rome, I thought every Roman a knave*	**Donec** (*or* **antequam**) Romam veni, Romanos omnes veteratores esse duxi
UNTIL *I* (POSSIBILITY) *am deceived, I shall treat him as though he were honest*	Hominem, donec me **deceperit**, tanquam probum habebo
I shall NOT *believe you* UNTIL *you keep your word*	Quum promissa **servabis, tum demum** tibi credam

WHEN, see the beginning of the Paragraph.

WHILE *this was going on, the enemy fled*	Dum hæc **geruntur** (not **gerebantur**) hostes terga dederunt (Par. 11)
WHILE HEADING *a charge, he fell*	**Dum** pugnam princeps **ciet**, occidit. (Or **ciens** rarely ; but never **dum ciens**. See Par. 70.)

The sequence of events is sometimes expressed in English by the Present Participle of the Verb *have*. '*Having* finished this, i.e. *having* this finished, I shall return.' This is rendered in Latin by the Pass. Part. Abl. Absolute, 'his auditis,' or by a Conjunction.

N.B.—With Intransitive Verbs, the Ablative Absolute cannot be used : '*Having* now settled here, I don't intend to move.' '**Quoniam** hic jam **consedi**, migrare nolo.'

None but the Deponent Participles can render the English Participle with *having*, e.g. '*having* said this he departed,' 'hæc **locutus** abiit.'

Examples: **Adeptus, amplexus, arbitratus, ausus, expertus, functus, hortatus, mortuus, nactus, oblitus, ortus, passus, questus, ratus, solitus, testatus, ultus, usus.**

67. Conjunctions of circumstance.

We say virtue is the chief object of life, WHEREAS *or* WHILE *you say pleasure is*	Virtutem nos quidem, **vos autem** voluptatem summum bonum esse dicitis

N.B.—Distinguish this use of *while* from the temporal use. *Autem* is often omitted.

It is unjust that this should be granted to you WHILE *it is refused to us*	Injustum est hoc vobis concedi, negari nobis

68. Conjunctions of reason are followed by the Indicative, if prominence is given to the truth of the *fact* on which some statement is based.

AS *you have promised, you must keep your word*	Tu, **quoniam** promisisti, fidem præstare debes
IN THAT *you did it knowingly, your crime is worse than that of the rest*	**Quod** (or Tu **qui**) sciens fecisti, gravius quam ceteri, peccavisti

N.B.—When we put *not* before *because*, the Verb following *not because* very often expresses something that is not a *fact*. Hence:

I do this, not BECAUSE *it's pleasant, but* BECAUSE *it's right*	Hoc facio, non **quod** jucundum **sit**, sed **quia** honestum **est**

But, even where *fact* is expressed, the Subjunctive is used, if there is a *thought*, e.g. of cause:

INASMUCH AS (SEEING THAT, SINCE) *you do not pity us, you cannot expect us to pity you*	Tu, **quum** (*or* **qui**) nostri non **miserearis**, non sperare debes fore ut tui misereamur.
I ought to be grateful INASMUCH AS *I have received many benefits from him*	Debeo gratus esse, **ut qui** multa ab illo beneficia **acceperim**
SINCE *this is so, why do we delay?*	Quæ **quum** ita **sint**, cur moramur?

69. Conjunctions of condition.

In a language that, like Latin, has distinct Moods to denote *fact* and *not fact*, **si**, when followed by the Present or Past Tense of the Indicative, loses the exact notion of condition, and must mean either (1) *when*, as in '**si** quando **vidit**' or (2) 'assuming, for a moment, as a fact,' *e.g.* '**Si** nihil aliud **fecerunt**, satis præmii habent.' So '**si** Deus mundum **creavit**,' '*assuming that* God created the world.'

This (2) use of the Indicative leaves it an open question whether, *in the writer's opinion*, the Verb expresses a *fact* or not. The Subjunctive distinctly expresses what is *not fact*, though it may be hereafter *fact:* that is to say, the Subjunctive after **si** expresses what is genuinely, and the Indicative Past and Present after **si** what is fictitiously, conditional.

The following are genuine conditional sentences:—

IF* *I (shall find that I)* HAVE *anything, I will give it*	**Si** quid **habebo**, dabo. (Note the English weakness, *have* being used both for Future and Present)
Should I have (or, if I were to have, or, if I had, which is possible) anything, I would give it	**Si** quid **habeam**, dem

* *If* in 'I don't know *if*' means *whether*. See 53.

IF *I had anything (which I have not, and cannot have) I would give it*	Si quid **haberem, darem**
IF *I had had anything, I would have given it*	Si quid **habuissem, dedissem.** (Or, graphically, **dederam**)

Rule—In conditional sentences, 'si' with the Past Tenses of the Subjunctive is used to denote an impossible, 'si' with the Present Tenses, to denote a possible, condition.

Sometimes the thought is changed from *sequence* to *consequence*, in which case the Verb is changed in the Apodosis,* from the Future to the Present Subjunctive, *e.g.* 'Si quid habebo, dem,' 'if I have anything, I *will*, or *rather*, I *would*, give it.' But this is not common except in silver Latin. And:

Rule—The Subjunctives in the Protasis and the Apodosis, must be both Present or both Past.†

IF NOT: see Paragraph 70.

You will succeed, PROVIDED THAT *you do your best*	Rem perficies **dummodo** (or **modo si** or **modo**) pro virili **agas**
SUPPOSING *I have a dagger, it does not follow that I'm an assassin*	**Fac** me sicam **habere;** non sum continuo sicarius (*or* Etiam **si** sicam habeo, *assuming it as a fact*)

A condition can also be expressed by a Participle or Ablative Absolute, provided there is no ambiguity.

* The 'if' clause is called the *Antecedent* or *Protasis*; the clause containing the consequence is called the *Consequent* or *Apodosis*.
† The Imperfect may correspond to the Pluperfect), *e.g.* 'tu, si mihi **paruisses,** non nunc Romae **esses**': but you could not have '**pareas, esses,**' '**pareres, sis.**'

IF *you take the city in three months, what will you do then?*	Quid igitur deinde facies, **urbe** tribus his mensibus **capta?**

But if '**tribus his mensibus**' were removed, the meaning might be 'since you have taken the city.'

Though (O.E. *theah*) is connected with *the, that*; and calls attention to a condition or circumstance 'even *in the* (case that).' The close connection between the Demonstrative and Relative (*the* was once the English Relative, as *that* now is) makes it not surprising that *though*, i.e. *in-the*, or *al-though*, i.e. *even in the*, should be rendered in Latin by **quanquam** (quam-quam), or **quamvis**, both emphatic forms of **quam**, *in the way in which*, or *in what way*. **Quanquam** often refers to facts, '**quanquam** iratus est,' '*although* he is angry;' **quamvis** (in the best prose) means *however much*, and does not refer to a definite fact. Hence :

Rule—' Quanquam ' generally takes the Indicative, ' quamvis ' never (in good Prose).

Rule—' Quamvis ' is often used with Adjectives, without a Verb :

Pray be silent, however angry you may be	**Quamvis iratus,** cura ut taceas

Though often implies that something does not exist *in the way in which* it might be expected to. Hence :

THOUGH *he is brave, he's not very clever*	Homo est, **ut** fortis, **ita** non admodum acutus (*In the way wherein, or whereas, he's brave, &c*)

The same sentence might be expressed thus, ' He is brave, but *in such a way that* he's not clever,' ' **Ita** fortis **est ut** tamen non acutus sit.'

THOUGH *this is useful, it is not right*	Hoc est **ita** utile **ut** honestum non sit

Though, used parenthetically for *yet*, *but*, is **quanquam**.

THOUGH, *why do I waste time in complaining?*	**Quanquam,** cur querendo tempus tero?

Unless, if . . . . *not,* **nisi :** rarely **si non,** unless the **si** and **non** are separated. **Nisi** follows the same rule as **si**. See above.

'*Not* . . . . *unless*' is sometimes represented in Latin by '**ita** . . . . **si**,' i.e. '*only on this condition* . . . . *if.*'

I shall not forgive you UNLESS *you forgive him*	Ego, **hac lege** (*or* **ita**) tibi, **si** tu illi, ignoveris
UNLESS *you agree in your wishes, you cannot be friends*	Quod **si** eadem velitis, **tum demum** amicitiam possitis conjungere. (*Then and not till then*)

Whether (*which of two*) is often equivalent in English to *if on the one hand*. '*Whether* (i.e. *whichever of two things we do*) *we rejoice or sorrow, we shall always remember you*.' This is rendered in Latin by **sive**, *if either*, '*Nos*, **sive** *gaudebimus*, **sive** (or **seu**) *dolebimus, tui nunquam obliviscemur*.'

N.B.—Carefully distinguish between *whether* meaning *whichever of two things*, **sive,** and *whether* following a Verb, *e.g.* 'he asked,' and meaning *which of two* things, i.e. **utrum**. (See Paragraph 51.)

<small>The principal danger of confusing the two meanings of *whether* is, when *whether* means **sive**, but is placed after the principal sentence, *e.g.* 'I am not much annoyed, *whether* this be true or false.'</small>

N.B.—Note here that, though in English we sometimes use *be* after *whether*, the Latins, as in the last example, use the Indicative. The reason is that *nothing is implied as to the possible incorrectness of the suppositions:* the meaning is 'assuming it to be true, or assuming it to be false, and I'm not just now concerned with the question whether it is true or false.'

70. English Ellipsis of Verb after Conjunctions. We have seen that **quamvis** can be used Adverbially to qualify an Adjective or Participle. In English a great number of Conjunctions are thus used, '*while* walking' for '*while* he was walking.' So, '*when* young,' '*though* hot-tempered,' '*if* true.' This ellipsis is rare in Latin. Insert the Verb, *e.g.* 'when he *was* young,' or turn the sentence by an. appositional Noun, or by a qualifying Participle, or otherwise:

WHILE WALKING *he fell*	**Ambulans, dum ambulat,** cecidit
WHEN A BOY *Balbus was sent to Athens*	**Balbus puer** Athenas missus est
He is frivolous, IF NOT *immoral*	Homo levis est, **nedum** (*or* **ne dicam**) improbus

71. Conjunctions of result. Even in English we sometimes express *result* (even though it is a *fact*) not as a *fact*, but as a *consequence*, in the Infinitive. 'The walls were so battered as *to* be no longer tenable.' The Latins, having their Subjunctive, express a result by that Mood, preceded by **ut**, *in which way*, **quut, quo**(d), old Abl. of **qui**. Sometimes **ut** is preceded by **ita**, *in that way*.

N.B.—This construction* is used even after verbs of happening, the notion perhaps being 'things happened *in such a way that, &c.*' *e.g.* 'It happened once that the house was set on fire.' 'Forte accidit **ut** ædes **incenderentur.**'

72. Conjunctions of purpose. Purpose is expressed in Latin by (1) **ut** with the Subjunctive, (2) **ad** with the Gerund or Gerundive, and, more rarely, (3) **causa** preceded by the Gerund or Gerundive, and (4) the Fut. Part. Active; also, after Verbs of Motion by (5) the Supine, *e.g.* 'venio **visum** urbem,' where **visum** is really a Verbal Noun placed in the Acc. after **venio** (like **rus, domum**), and itself governing an Accusative.

* When using it, observe the Sequence of Tenses, 64.

N.B.—In Construction (1), which is by far the most common, be careful to observe the Sequence of Tenses.

I have come THAT *I may take the city*   Veni (1) **ut capiam**, (2) **ad capiendam**, (3) **capiendi causa**, (4) **capturus**, (5) **captum**, urbem

We have seen above (Paragraph 45) that the Latins like to give prominence to a Negative, *e.g.* **nisi** for *if . . . not*. In the same way:

Rule—'That . . . not' denoting purpose is generally represented by 'ne,' or more rarely 'ut . . . ne': and so, instead of 'ut nemo,' you should write 'ne quis'; instead of 'ut nunquam,' 'ne quando.'*

O that! is rendered in Latin by **utinam**, '(I desire) *that indeed*, &c.' *e.g.* '**utinam** veniat,' '(I desire) *that* he may *indeed* come.' Wishes about the past are useless. Hence

Rule—'Utinam' with the Present Subjunctive introduces wishes that can be, with the Past Subjunctive, wishes that cannot be, realized.

73. '**To**,' **various meanings of.** *To* presents many difficulties to the beginner. Take for example, 'I eat *to* live.' Here 'to live' is not a Present Infinitive by derivation. It used to be 'to livene,' where *to* meant *toward*, and *livene (living)* was a Gerund, *e.g.* 'I eat *to live*' = 'I eat *toward living*.' Hence :

Rule—Whenever 'to' before a verb denotes purpose, it is not to be translated by the Latin Infinitive.

* This applies only to *that* followed by *may, might*, and denoting *purpose*

I eat TO LIVE	Vescor { vivendi causa / ut vivam / ad vivendum
I come TO SEE	Venio { visum / visurus

When therefore is *to live* to be rendered **vivere**? Only when * *to live* is really a Noun and means *living*, as:

I should like TO LIVE	Velim **vivere**
TO LIVE *is pleasant*	**Vivere** jucundum est

Now take 'I promise *to come.*' That means 'I promise *coming.*' Yes, but the coming is future; and though we have no Future Participle, the Latins have, and can say 'I promise myself *to be about to come.*'

Rule—After 'I hope,' 'I promise,' turn 'to' by the Latin Future Participle Active.

I promise, hope, to come	Promitto, spero, me **venturum**
I determine, propose, to come	{ Statuo, in animo mihi est, **venire** / *But also*, Constituo me **venturum**

N.B.—'I hope *that* it *is* so' = 'spero rem ita se **habere.**'

Sometimes, where *to* conveys to our ears no distinct notion of purpose, nor of consequence, the Latins seem to find the notion:

I determine TO (IN SUCH A WAY *that I may*) *come*	Constituo **ut** veniam

---

* Here the *to* is redundant, improperly added as the sign of the Inf. *To*, in Early English, was used like *ad* in Latin, before the Gerund. The similarity of the Inf. *liven* to the Gerund *livene* (which was a Dative form) caused the two to be confused; and, inflections being lost, the *to* was improperly transferred to the Inf., even when there was no notion of purpose.

The best kind of worship is TO *worship (such that we worship) God with purity of mind*	Cultus deorum optimus est **ut** eos pura mente veneremur
It is the way with men TO *envy their superiors*	Mos est hominum **ut** superioribus invideant. (Their custom is *such that, &c.*)

'I happened *to* see him' seems to be a confusion between '*I happened, happed,* or *lighted* on seeing him,' and '*it happened* to me to see him.' The Latins use the latter construction with **ut**, 'contigit mihi **ut** hominem viderem.'

Rule—Use 'ut' after 'contingit,' 'accidit,' 'evenit,' 'fit,' &c.

N.B.—After verbs of *asking, commanding, advising,* and *striving, to* is rendered by **ut** with the Subjunctive. It is easy to see that, in 'I command you to go,' *to go* may be regarded as independent of what precedes, and as equivalent to '*in order that* you may go,' 'impero tibi **ut eas**'; or else *you-to-go* may be regarded as an Objective clause, '*your going*,' after '*I* command,' 'jubeo **te ire**.' Hence:

Rule—
With *ask, command, advise* and *strive,*
By **ut** translate Infinitive;
But not so after **jubeo**, nor
After the Verb Deponent **conor**.

To after an Adjective modified by *enough*, e.g. *not good enough*, or after *fit, worthy*, conveys a notion of purpose or result, and may therefore be rendered by **ut** or by **qui** (*i.e.* **ut is**) with the Subjunctive.

He is not fit for you TO *converse with*	Non dignus est **quocum** (i.e. **ut** cum eo) colloquaris

The Adjective is sometimes implied in *the:*

I am not the (SUITABLE) *man* TO *commit such a fault*	Non is sum **qui** (**ut ego**) hanc culpam admittam

To denoting purpose and following the Object* of a Transitive Verb, is often rendered by the Relative followed by the Subjunctive.

I sent men TO *ask for peace*	Misi (homines) **qui** (*i.e.* **ut ii**) pacem peterent

To after *too* is expressed, in Latin, by a periphrasis. 'He is too kind *to* hate' means '*for the purpose of* hating, he is too kind.' But the expression is slovenly and liable to ambiguity. What is the meaning of:

'Too fond *to* rule alone'?—POPE.†

It might mean 'too foolishly affectionate to rule alone,' but it is intended to mean 'too fond of ruling.' To avoid the ambiguity that might attend such sentences as 'nimis clemens est ut irascatur *or* ad irascendum,' the Latins say, 'he is kinder *than that he could* (or, *than a man that could*) be angry.' 'Clementior est **quam ut** *or* **quam qui** possit odisse.'

They came too late TO *be of any use*	Serius advenere **quam qui** possent prodesse

To often means '*as regards*'‡ in (1) 'He was the first *to*,' (2) 'I am glad *to*,' 'I am sorry *to*,' &c. In (1) *is, was*, &c. is inserted for emphasis in English, but is not required in Latin. In (2) *to* is rendered by **quod**, or sometimes, as

---

* The Object is sometimes understood in Latin.

† Compare

'but, for a calm unfit,
Would steer *too* nigh the sands *to* boast his wit.'
DRYDEN.

‡ '*To sue* to live, I find I seek to die,
And *seeking* death find life.'
Measure for Measure, iii. 1. 43.

Here, *to sue* means *in suing*, and corresponds to *seeking*.— *Shakespearian Grammar*, Paragraph 357.

in (1), the English Infinitive becomes the Latin principal Verb.

Cato was the first TO *speak* Cato **primus dixit**
I was glad TO *find that you were in good health* Gaudebam **quod** te intellexi bene valere, *or*, **libenter** intellexi

To also means *as regards* or *in*, after *shameful, wonderful, incredible, easy, pleasant, honourable,* and is sometimes rendered by the so-called Passive Supine, *e.g.* 'mirabile **dictu**,' 'wonderful *in*-the-saying.'

Dictu, factu, gustatu, auditu, cognitu, visu, inventu, and others are thus used.

74. The English Present Participle often expresses more than mere simultaneousness, and therefore cannot often be rendered by the Latin Present Participle. It often implies some Conjunction; but what Conjunction is implied, it is not always easy to determine. The loose and ambiguous use of the Present Participle is a defect in English.

N.B.—The meaning of the Participle must be determined by the context. When the Principal Verb is in the Past or Present Tense, the Participle often means 'although' or 'since'; when the Principal Verb is in the Future Tense, the Participle often means 'if.' This also applies to Verbals preceded by Prepositions: see Par. 75.

KNOWING (SINCE YOU KNOW) *this, why do you ask more questions?* Quæ **quum scias** cur plura quæris?

KNOWING (ALTHOUGH HE KNEW) *that it had been forbidden, he nevertheless ventured to come* **Quamvis sciret** id vetitum esse, ausus est tamen venire

FINDING (AS SOON AS, *or,* IF *he finds*) *that he is unwelcome, he will return* Hic **simul atque** (*or* si modo) **intellexerit** se haud expectatum venire, redibit

Sciens would mean simply 'in the state of knowing,' or 'at the time of knowing.'

The Relative is often to be supplied before a Participle in English, *e.g.* 'the soldiers (that were) *remaining* in the town, as well as those (that were) *encamped* outside.' This Relative must be expressed in Latin. (See Par. 58.)

75. The English Verbal gives great flexibility to our language. It is a great advantage to be able, by merely affixing *-ing*, to construct an abstract Noun out of any Verb. The English Verbals *have very few corresponding* Latin Verbals, *e.g.* **tactus,** *touching;* **auditus, equitatio** (Pliny).

When the English Verbal is the Subject or Object, it is often equivalent to an Infinitive:

WALKING *is healthier; but I prefer* RIDING   Quamvis **ambulare** mihi plus prosit, malo tamen **equitare**

We cannot say (though Shakespeare could), '*the* taking a city.' Why not? Because *the*, to our ears, converts the Verbal into a mere Noun, requiring *of* after it. In the same way the Latins could not say 'venio ad visum urbem,' because the **ad** made **visum** too much like a Noun. They therefore omitted **ad**. For the same reason they did not like to say 'ad videndum urbem.' But in this case, instead of omitting **ad** to retain the Verbal force of **videndum,** they retain **ad** and change **videndum** into the Adjective **videndam.**

When the Gerund is governed, not by a Preposition, but by a Noun, *e.g.* 'consilium videndi,' the Genitive (which may be either Possessive or Objective) does not, like a Preposition, *Nounify* the Gerund so as to prevent it from having its Verbal force. We can therefore write either '**urbem videndi,** or **urbis videndæ** consilium.'

Rule—After Prepositions, if the Verb has an Object, use the Gerundive and not the Gerund, *e.g.* 'in victore (not -em) laudando.'

VERBALS.

The Gerund (or Gerundive, if combined with a Substantive) follows **ad**, *for;* **de**, *concerning;* **in**, *in;* **ob**, *on account of;* rarely **inter**, and *other Prepositions.*

Note the different renderings of the same Preposition and Verbal, varying with the difference of Tense in the principal Verb.

Verbals after Prepositions.

I have no doubt ABOUT *your* RECOVERING	Non dubito **quin** futurum sit ut convalescas
Write to him ABOUT PARDONING *the prisoners*	Fac scribas homini **de** venia captivis danda
AS TO FORGIVING *him, I shall do no such thing*	**Quod** me rogas (rogant) ut ignoscam homini, omnino non faciam
I am surprised AT *your* OBJECTING	Miror **quod** adversaris
He's clever AT FINDING *weak points*	Satis acutus est **in** investigandis erroribus
BESIDES SINGING *she can dance*	Mulier **non solum canit** sed etiam saltare didicit
What do you mean BY THREATENING *me?*	Quid vis **quod** mihi hæc minaris?
BY BREAKING *down the bridge, he cut off the supplies of the enemy*	**Ponte rescisso** hostem a commeatu **interclusit**
BY GETTING *up early, I expect to finish my work*	**Si** prima luce **surrexero**, spero me opus perfecturum
One gains style BY READING *speeches and poems*	Elegantia loquendi **legendis oratoribus** et poetis augetur
BY PERSEVERING *he won*	**Perseverando** vicit
DURING *the* BUILDING *of the bridge*	**Inter faciendum** pontem

I shall punish you FOR DOING *this*	Te, **qui** hoc feceris, pœna afficiam
Socrates was condemned FOR CORRUPTING, *so people said, the young men*	Socrates damnatus est **quod** juventutem corrumperet (Subjunctive expresses 'so people said')
You have no cause FOR COMPLAINING	Non habes **cur queraris**
The ram was useful FOR BATTERING *down the wall*	Aries utilis erat **ad muros conquassandos**
It's a shame to take money FOR GIVING *a verdict*	Turpe est pecuniam **ob rem judicandam** accipere
I was deterred by him FROM COMING	Hic me **quominus venirem** deterruit
FROM EQUIVOCATING *you will come* TO LYING	Tergiversatus mox mentieris / Tergiversatio mendacii parens
HOPING *is very different* FROM BELIEVING	**Sperare** aliud, aliud et dissimillimum est **credere**
IN KEEPING *your word you will be consulting your brother's interests*	**Si fidem præstiteris** / **Fidem præstando** } fratri consules
You are late IN COMING	**Sero venis**
IN DOING *this I have no object but the good of the country*	**Quod** autem **hoc facio** nullam habeo causam præter rei-publicæ commodum
Virtue is manifested IN DESPISING *pleasure*	**In contemnenda voluptate** virtus cernitur
IN BLAMING *him you blame me*	**Quum** illum culpas, me quoque culpas
I am IN FAVOUR OF RETREATING	Equidem **recedendum esse** censeo

INSTEAD OF CRYING *you laugh*	**Tantum abest ut** lacrimeris, ut rideas Rides **quum debeas** lacrimari
INSTEAD OF CRYING, *work*	Age, **omissis lacrymis,** tenta quid possis
This comes OF HELPING *you*	**Quod** tibi **subvenire volui** hunc habeo fructum
I am tired OF HEARING *the same thing a thousand times*	Tædet me eadem milliens **audire**
The idea OF *your ever* IMPROVING!	Tu **ut** unquam te corrigas! (i.e. *to suppose that, &c.*)
I despair OF FINDING *it*	Despero me id **reperturum esse**
ON HEARING *this he blushed*	**His auditis** } erubuit **Quæ quum audivisset** }
What will you do ON HEARING *this?*	**Quæ si intellexeris** **Simul atque hæc intellexeris** } quid tandem facies?
He is bent ON MAKING *money*	Attentus est **ad divitias accumulandas**
SINCE HEARING *from you I found that I was mistaken*	**Postquam** tuas literas **accepi,** intellexi me errorem fecisse
SINCE SETTING OUT *from home, I have not received one letter*	Litteras, **ex quo tempore** domo **profectus sum,** ne singulas quidem accepi
He failed THROUGH ATTEMPTING *too much*	Ne modica quidem tenuit, **quia** ad altiora **tendebat**
No one ever sees him WITHOUT *calling him a traitor*	Nemo illum unquam adspicit **quin** proditorem compellet

He speaks well WITHOUT PERSUADING *anybody*	Bene loquitur, **neque** tamen cuiquam persuadet
You will make mischief WITHOUT *meaning it*	**Quamvis** imprudens, certamina seres
I should not have come here WITHOUT *obtaining a safe conduct*	Quod **nisi** mihi hostis fidem dedisset tuto me rediturum, nunquam huc venissem
He was condemned WITHOUT BEING *heard*	**Inauditus** damnatus est
WITHOUT *openly accusing him you insinuate charges against him*	**Ita** hominem non accusas **ut** tamen operte insimules
We returned WITHOUT EFFECTING *anything*	**Re infecta,** rediimus

N.B.—The Gerundive, *e.g.* **ferendum**, means, in Cicero, 'that which *is to be, ought to be,* borne.' In later writers, it sometimes means 'that which *may be, can be,* borne.' But, *when preceded by* **non** *or* **vix, ferendum** is used even by Cicero, to mean *bearable, tolerable.*

76. The Subject of the principal Verb, in a sentence containing a subordinate sentence, should often come first in Latin, where it does not come first in English:

When THEMISTOCLES *had secured the safety of Greece by the destruction of the Persian fleet, he wrote a letter to Xerxes*	**Themistocles,** postquam, Persarum classe deleta, Græciam servavit, epistolam ad Xerxen misit

Thus the clumsy repetition of *he* is avoided.

77. Parentheses. The introduction of a Pronoun may sometimes be avoided, and the unity of the sentence and prominence of the principal Subject may still be preserved, by the use of a parenthesis. This is very commonly used to describe some minute circumstance connected with the principal Subject or Object :

He accordingly gave orders to the whole army to march to Nuceria. IT *was about ten miles off.*	Itaque suis imperavit ut Nuceriam—**aberat autem fere decem millia passuum**—cum omnibus copiis contenderent.

If the clause had not been introduced parenthetically, immediately after **Nuceria**, so as to avoid the possibility of ambiguity, **illa** or **oppidum** would have been of necessity inserted.

78. In Oratio Recta the words of the speaker are used.
The usual method of introducing a speech in Oratio Recta is to leave the previous sentence unfinished, supplying the verb **inquit** (not **dixit** nor **respondebat**) *after the first emphatic word of the speech.*

Then Crassus SAID '*I for my part don't believe it*'	Tum Crassus 'Equidem' **inquit** ' non credo '
Why not?' *I* ANSWERED	Cui ego 'Quare' **inquam** 'non credis?'

Sometimes **inquit** is omitted, the previous sentence being still left incomplete. 'Tum Crassus "Equidem non credo."'

78a. In Oratio Obliqua, *that* must be placed before the English words of the speaker, which are consequently changed in person and tense. *Crassus said that he did not believe it.*
The following changes take place in Latin. The first is so obviously necessary that it requires no reason :

(*a*) Rule—All principal Verbs (that is, Verbs directly making a statement) are transformed from the Indicative to the Infinitive, retaining their original Tenses.

H

(*He said*) '*I* DON'T BE-LIEVE *it*, *I never* DID *believe it, and I never* SHALL *believe it*'	(Dixit) 'se neque * **credere** neque **credidisse** neque unquam **crediturum**'

Notice that there is no change in Latin to correspond to the English change from the Present in Oratio Recta to the Past in Oratio Obliqua, 'I *do* not believe,' 'He said that he *did* not believe.' In Latin the Verbs, though changed in Mood, *retain their original Tenses*. The Latin language has not the English power of representing the Simple Past after **dixit**. 'Negavit se **credidisse**' would mean 'He said that he *had not believed*,' i.e. in Oratio Recta 'I *have* not believed.' Remember therefore to translate : '*He said that he* DID *not believe*' by 'Negavit se **credere**.'

The Future Infinitive does not exist in all Latin Verbs, *e.g.* not in most Inceptives, such as **mitesco, crebresco, cresco**. We must therefore use a periphrasis

He said that (IT WOULD COME TO PASS THAT) *the city would increase*	Dixit **fore ut** urbs cresceret

Remember that the Passive Future Infinitive, **captum iri**, means 'that there is a going to capture,' **captum** being an indeclinable Supine. Consequently **captum** cannot agree with **urbem** in :

He said that the city WOULD BE TAKEN	Dixit urbem **captum iri**

Conditional Tenses of the Apodosis (page 83, note) that are in the Subjunctive in O. Recta, are rendered by the Fut. Partic. with **esse** or **fuisse** in O. Obliqua:

---

* These words are supposed to come in the middle of a speech at a distance from **dixit**: if they were close to **dixit**, you would have **negavit** for **dixit neque**.

Oratio Recta.	Oratio Obliqua.
Ad hæc Cæsar: 'Si' inquit 'intra decimum diem urbem tradidissetis equidem ab oppugnandis muris **temperavissem**'	Ad hæc Cæsar respondit: 'Se, si intra decimum diem urbem tradidissent, ab oppugnandis muris **temperaturum fuisse**'
Si modo' inquit 'frater mihi adesset, **gauderem**'	'Si frater sibi adesset, se **gavisurum fuisse**.' (Unfulfilled condition)
'Si quid' inquit 'habeam, dem'	'Se, si quid **haberet daturum esse**.' (Fulfilment of condition possible)

(*b*) In the Oratio Obliqua, the writer does not guarantee any statement of the speaker as a *fact*, and therefore has no right to use the Indicative. Note therefore the following changes :—

Oratio Recta.	Oratio Obliqua.
Tum alter 'Misi' inquit 'servos quos **habui** fidelissimos'	'Se misisse servos quos (*in his opinion*) fidelissimos **haberet**'
Cui Balbus 'Veniam' inquit 'si **potero**, quanquam hodie **ægroto**; sin minus, veniet frater, qui decem tantum millia passuum **abest**'	'Se venturum, si **posset**, quanquam illo die **ægrotaret**; sin minus, venturum fratrem, qui decem tantum millia passuum **abesset**'
Ille respondens 'Si' inquit 'Cicero **occisus erit**, omnes moriemur'	'Si Cicero **occisus esset**, se omnes morituros esse'

Rule—Subordinate Indicatives, that is, Indicatives following 'qui,' 'quia,' 'quam,' 'quanquam,' 'quum,' 'etsi,' 'si,' in Oratio Recta, are changed into Subjunctives in Oratio Obliqua.

Where **qui=et is, nam is,** it is sometimes followed by the Infinitive in Oratio Obliqua: thus '**qui** abest' in the last example but one, above, might have been rendered in Oratio Obliqua by '**quem (nam eum)** abesse.'
Beginners had better not use this licence.

(*c*) Put *he said that*, before an Imperative, e.g. *run*, **licet curras, fac curras.** *Run* will then have to be changed into *he ought to run*, **currendum esse**, or *he might, should, run* (**licere ut**) **curreret**, (**faciendum esse ut**) **curreret.** Hence :

The general cried, '*Press on, do not give ground.*'

Oratio Recta.	Oratio Obliqua.
Imperator '**Instate**' inquit, '**nolite** pedem referre'	Imperator milites hortatur (*Hist. Pres.*) ' **Instarent, nollent** pedem **referre**,' *i.e.* 'let them press on.'

Rule—Imperatives in Oratio Recta are to be turned into Imperfect Subjunctives in Oratio Obliqua.

(*d*) A question in the Second Person, *e.g.* 'What are you doing?' may naturally become a Dependent Interrogative, when preceded by *he said*, which implies *he asked*. Thus:

'*Why are you advancing? Why did you not sound the retreat?*'	'**Cur progrederentur?** Cur non receptui **cecinissent?**'

Rule—Questions in the Second Person are to be rendered in the Oratio Obliqua by the Imperfect or Pluperfect Subjunctive.

Questions, being asked about oneself, or about an absent person, are very often not asked for information, but to express emotion. They are then called *questions* of **appeal.** If 'Why do I delay?' were rendered in Oratio Obliqua '(interrogavit) cur moraretur,' it would seem too formal and frigid, as though it were a question really asked for information. Hence the Latins prefer to render such passionate questions by the Infinitive. 'He said *he was delaying there*—(and) *why?*' '**Cur se morari?**

'Why are we lingering here? Why is our general absent?'   'Cur **se** ibi **morari**? Cur **abesse** imperatorem?'

The Future Indicative must be rendered by the Future Infinitive :

'WILL *the enemy* DELAY?'   'Num **hostem moraturum esse**?'

Rule—Questions in the First and Third Person are to be rendered in the Oratio Obliqua by the Accusative of the Person, and the Infinitive of the Verb.

(*e*) **Pronouns, Personal and Demonstrative, together with** their derived Adverbs, will usually be changed.

Of course **ego, tu, nos,** and **vos** cannot possibly find a place in Oratio Obliqua; **me** must be changed into **se, tu** into **ille,** &c. Further, 'I stand *here*,' said he, 'for justice,' will be changed into 'He said that he stood *there* for justice.' Thus, **hic** will be changed into **ille, nunc** into **tum, hic** (adv.) into **ibi**; and **hodie** would be regularly changed into **illo die**. But, for vividness' sake, the demonstrative forms may sometimes be retained.

(*f*) *He, him, his,* are often ambiguous in an English speech reported (as in newspapers) in Oratio Obliqua. The Latin distinction between **se** and **illum** diminishes but does not remove the ambiguity.

The general rule is that **se** refers to the speaker, thus ·

'*Let them not distrust his watchfulness*'   'Ne de **sua** vigilantia dubitarent'

But, when **suus** is wanted to refer to the Subject of some subordinate Verb, *e.g.* of **dubitarent** above, then **ipse** is sometimes used *antithetically* to refer to the speaker, thus :

'*Let them not distrust their own valour or his watchfulness*'	'Ne de **sua** virtute aut de **ipsius** vigilantia desperarent'

At other times, the **ipse** emphasizes a subordinate Subject to shew that **suus, se** refer to that Subject, and not to the principal Subject.

He said '*he (the speaker) advised him to save himself*'	'Se monere illum ut **se ipse** servaret'

(*g*) The sentence preceding a speech in Oratio Obliqua is often completed, and the speech begun with the Verb of speaking implied and not expressed. 'Imperator in hunc modum milites hortabatur. "Instarent; quid morarentur? Præsto esse victoriam."'

The following is an example of the differences between Oratio Recta and Oratio Obliqua :—

Oratio Recta.	Oratio Obliqua.
Imperator, milites hortatus '**Instate**' inquit. '**Cur nunc hic moramur**? Num hostis **morabitur**? **Nolite** dubitare de **vestra** virtute aut de **mea** vigilantia. Si ignavus **fuissem, vos deseruissem, urbs** enim, ut opinor, non facile **capietur**, neque frigoris **vis mitescet.** Sed **nolo** ignavia vitam emere. Quod imperatorem **decuit** id **perfeci;** quod si pro patria **moriar,** mortem non invitus **oppetam**'	Imperator milites in hunc modum hortabatur. '**Instarent.** Cur **tum se ibi morari**? Num **hostem moraturum esse**? Nollent de **sua v**irtute aut de **ipsius** vigilantia dubitare. Si ignavus fuisset, se **illos deserturum fuisse : urbem** enim, (**sic se opinari**) non facile **captum iri,** neque fore ut frigoris **vis mitesceret.** Sed **nolle** (se) ignavia vitam emere. Quod imperatorem **deceret,** id se **perfecisse :** quod si pro patria **moreretur,** mortem non **invitum oppetiturum**'

79. Metaphors.

An English Metaphor, e.g. *this thought struck me*, need not, and often cannot, be rightly translated literally into Latin. To say (as Quintilian says) **feriit**, would mean *forcibly impressed*, whereas we wish to convey little more than *suggested itself, occurred to* me. The right translation would be 'hoc mihi **in mentem venit**.'

Many English words and expressions are metaphorical, though we use them so commonly that we have almost forgotten the latent metaphor, *e.g.* 'at its *height*,' 'on the *point* of,' 'on the *ground* that,' 'the *scene* (i.e. stage) of his disgrace,' 'at this *juncture, stage*.' Many other recognized Metaphors can be rendered by other Latin Metaphors, *but not literally.*

The pupil must gain, by observation and practice, the power of rightly rendering English Metaphors into Latin. The following are a few instances selected to shew metaphorical diversity in the two Languages :—

I am being TORTURED *and* WORN OUT *with sorrow*	**Lacerat** animum atque **exest** ægritudo
All the rest SPRINGS *from what has been mentioned before*	Ex his quæ dicta sunt reliqua **nascuntur** omnia
At all hazards, we must make everything SUBSERVIENT *to seeing this poor girl respectably married*	Quoquo modo se habebit, illius misellæ et matrimonio et famæ **serviendum erit**
They VENTED *their anger on me*	In me iram **profuderunt**
I maintain that there is an INFLUENCE *that may be exerted by God on men*	Dico esse quod a diis ad hominum vitam **permanare** possit
Sensual pleasure, you see, is TRANSITORY	**Fluit** igitur voluptas corporis

Greece SWARMS *with orators*	**Redundat** Græcia oratoribus
No one can APPROACH *Africanus in military distinction*	Nemo ad Africanum in militari laude **aspirare** potest. (Only with negatives classically used in this sense)
If it were expediency that KNITS *friends, a complete change of expediency would* PART *them*	Si utilitas **conglutinaret** amicos, eadem commutata **dissolveret**
When one's anger has COOLED	**Restinctis** jam animorum **incendiis**
The conspiracy is AT ITS HEIGHT	**Ardet** acerrime conjuratio
When matters GO ON *as we would have them*	Rebus ad voluntatem nostram **fluentibus**
Low though the laws are FALLEN, *yet they will one day* RISE	Leges, quamvis sint **demersæ, emergent** tamen aliquando
I BURY *myself in my books*	Literis me **involvo**
I AM KILLING TWO BIRDS WITH ONE STONE	Duos parietes de eadem fidelia dealbo. *Or*, Una mercede duas res assequor
The teaching of Pythagoras HAS SPREAD *even here*	Huc etiam **permanavit** Pythagoræ doctrina
Affection SPRINGING *from this origin gradually* DIFFUSES *itself abroad*	Caritas, hinc **nata, serpit** sensim foras
Mark what this kind of argument LEADS TO	Attende quo **serpat** hoc argumenti genus
The summer was WASTED	**Effluxit** æstas
I have been DEEPLY GRIEVED *by your two letters*	Binæ tuæ literæ valde me **momorderunt**

His character had been TAINTED, *or rather* BLASTED *by that condemnation*	Ex damnatione illa **semiustus**, vel potius **ambustus** evaserat
The musician did not TAKE THE FANCY OF *the people*	Tibicen **frigebat** ad populum (**friget** often means, *loses influence*)
I fear the ATTRACTION *of habit may prove too powerful for us*	Vereor ne **æstus** nos consuetudinis **absorbeat**
What a SEA *of evils!*	Quanta miseriarum **incendia**
These reminiscences have a sort of painful STING	Hæ recordationes **morsu** quodam dolorem efficiunt

It will be seen from the preceding examples that the simple Metaphors borrowed from *heat, cold, flowing, breathing, breaking*, &c. are more common in Latin than in English.

Latin is also more exuberant than English in the use of Metaphors. Note the use of different *Verbs* expressive of Metaphors, where in English we should use one Verb, sometimes varying the Metaphor in *Nouns*.

I have lived an honourable and prosperous life	**Viximus** honestissime, floruimus
As I hope to prosper, gentlemen, I can assure you that I have never allowed myself to be prevented from ministering to the necessities or interests of anyone, either by the attractions of leisure, or by the alluring voice of pleasure, or even by the necessity of sleep	Ita vivo, judices, ut a nullius unquam me tempore aut commodo, aut otium meum **abstraxerit**, aut voluptas **avocarit**, aut denique somnus **retardarit**

Compare the verbose English and the terse Latin in the following example :—

Give us a man that will not suffer himself to be worn out by petty annoyances, or prostrated by terror, a man that, in the pursuit of any object, will not give way to feverish desire, nor suffer his will to waste its strength in eager useless longings—and we have here the wise man that is the object of our search	Si quis nec **tabescat** molestiis, nec **frangatur** timore, nec sitienter quid expetens **ardeat** desiderio, nec alacritate futili gestiens **deliquescat**, is sit sapiens quem quærimus

The English is a great deal too verbose; and it would be more idiomatic though less literal to use *one Verb* and say, 'that will not give way to the feelings of petty irritation, or sudden terror, or feverish desire, or useless longing . . .'

<small>Personifications are more common in English than in Latin. "In English prose you might find a phrase like this, 'In the presence of purity so spotless, detraction hid its head, and envy ceased to whisper.' This way of speaking of ideas as if they were things . . . . is quite foreign to the simplicity and straightforwardness of Latin Prose."*</small>

80. Hyperbole, like Metaphor, must not always be literally rendered. For example, it does not follow, because we use *a thousand* to denote an indefinitely large number, that the Latins should use **mille**. It would be interesting to ascertain why they use **sexcenti** in the following example :

I prefer a *thousand* deaths   Malo **sexcenties** mori

---

* Bigg's *Easy Exercises in Latin Prose.*

MISCELLANEOUS IDIOMS.

MISCELLANEOUS IDIOMS.

I asked him to come to Rome	Rogavi illum ut Romam **veniret**
I have asked him to stop at Rome	Rogavi illum ut Romae **maneat**
When will you ask him to set out from Rome?	**Quando** illum rogabis ut **Roma proficiscatur?**
She is ten years old	Decem **annos nata est**
There are some who have said this was not true	Sunt qui **negaverint haec** vera **esse**
When a boy, I was charmed with this book	Hic liber mihi **puero** valde placuit. (Omit *When*)
They sent ambassadors to ask for peace	Legatos miserunt **qui** pacem **peterent**
You surely don't ask why we did this	Num rogas cur hoc **fecerimus?**
A slave of mine	Quidam e **servis meis**
I wrote, that you might hear the sooner	Scripsi, **quo** citius **intellegeres**
I shall soon know what you wish	Mox sciam **quid velis**
That wicked Tullius has caused me to despair	Tullius, **homo improbissimus**, effecit ut **desperem**. (Or, **improbus ille Tullius**)

The town of Corioli was taken	Corioli oppidum **captum est** (not **capti sunt**)
The heat was so great that almost all of us were unable to go on	Tantus erat calor ut fere omnes progredi non **possemus**
Why don't you enjoy what you've bought?	Cur non **emptis** frueris?
It is your interest that there should be peace; it is his that there should be war	**Tua** interest pacem, **illius** bellum esse
He threatens his own brother with death	Suo ipsius **fratri mortem** minatur
Ten days after the capture of Thebes	Decimo die post **captas Thebas**
I fear he will not come	**V**ereor ut veniat
I will teach you music	**Musicam** te docebo
You are being too much indulged	Nimis **tibi indulgetur**
Don't spare the prisoners	**Noli captivis** parcere. (Or, ne **peperceris,** but not ne **parcas** in prose)
I feared he would come too soon	Veritus sum **ne** citius **veniret**
He recommended his brother to escape	Fratri suo * ut **fugeret** suasit
He has recommended his own children to remain at Rome	Liberis suis suasit ut **Romæ maneant**
The celebrated Alexander	Alexander **ille**
Send me the most beautiful flowers you have	Cura ut **ad me** (*not* **mihi**) flores mittas, quos habeas pulcherrimos

* **Suo** may be omitted where the omission leaves no doubt whose **brother** is meant.

MISCELLANEOUS IDIOMS.

He reduced the Gauls to subjection	Gallos **suæ ditionis** fecit
In six days we came from Athens to Samos	**Sexto die Athenis Samum** venimus
What have I to do with you?	Quid **mihi tecum** est?
I shall go back to my home in Italy	Domum in **Italiam** redibo
There are some who hate me	Sunt qui me **oderint**
Having made this answer, he went home	**Hoc responso,** domum abiit
He came sooner than he was expected	**Opinione celerius** venit
He has long been desirous of death	Jamdudum mortem **optat**
Cæsar was killed by a friend	Cæsarem interfecit **amicus.** (Note the emphatic position of *amicus*, and the use of Latin Active for English Passive)
The battle took place in a narrow valley	In angusta valle **pugnatum est**
This was done by an enemy and not by chance	Hoc non casu sed **ab** inimico factum est. (**A** or **ab** with living agent)
He will see to the gathering of the flowers	Flores **carpendos** curabit
In front was the sea, in our rear the enemy	Mare **a** fronte, a tergo hostes imminebant. (Note the similarity of the Extremes and Means in a Latin Antithesis)
He made a long speech without persuading anyone to forgive him	Orationem longam **habuit, neque** tamen **ulli** persuasit ut sibi **ignosceret**

MISCELLANEOUS IDIOMS.

We shall set out from Carthage about the 7th of May	**Carthagine circiter Nonas Maias** proficiscemur
How many are there of you in London?	Quot **Londinii habitatis**?
Truth is the parent of what is expedient as well as of what is just	Veritas non **justi** solum sed etiam **utilitatis** mater est. (Not **utilis**, on account of the ambiguity)
Philosophy ought to have been your master	Philosophia tibi **magistra esse debuit**. (Not **magister**, because **Philosophia** is feminine)
I hoped you would be conquered	Speravi te **victum iri** or **fore ut vincereris**
It is not like a brave man to lose one's presence of mind	Non est **fortium** perturbari
I was the first to be asked to give an opinion	Ego primus rogatus sum **sententiam**
We ought not to have been kept in ignorance of this	Non debuimus **hoc** (**de hac re**) celari. (Note, the Noun requires **de**, the Neuter Pronoun does not)
I was somewhat disturbed by the shouts	Clamor me **nescio quid** perturbaverat
Three hundred of us are prepared to conquer or die	Trecenti **parati sumus** aut **ad vincendum** aut **ad moriendum**. (Not **paramur**)
I am persuaded that what you say is false	**Persuasum est mihi** te falsa dicere
He took and burned the bridge	Pontem **captum** incendit
It rarely happens that, &c.	**Raro** evenit ut, &c. (**Rare** = thinly, far apart)

MISCELLANEOUS IDIOMS.

My sister married his brother, and my brother his sister	Soror mea **fratri** ejus **nupsit**, frater autem sororem ejus **in matrimonium duxit**
When he performs a judge's duties rightly, then and not till then will he be worthy of praise	Hic, quum judicis munere recte **fungetur, tum demum laude** dignus erit
Has he been persuaded to speak the truth?	Num **ei persuasum est ut** vera **dicat**?
He imputed my virtue to me as a fault	Virtutem meam mihi **vitio** dedit
With you for our leader, we will not shrink even from famine	**Te duce, ne** famem **quidem** pertimescemus
She promises not to say one word	Promittit se **ne verbum quidem** emissuram esse
It is absolutely necessary for me to go	Necesse est **me ire**, *or*, Necesse est **eam**
No poet ever thought anyone superior to himself	**Nemo poeta** ullum* quam se meliorem putavit
He is the best jumper in the school	**Discipulorum, si quis alius, ille optime saltat**
I cannot help fearing	**Facere non possum** quin timeam
I am different from what I once was	Alius sum **atque** olim fui
The better you are (one is), the happier you are (one is)	{ Quo **quis** melior, eo beatior Ut **quisque** optimus, ita beatissimus
Hardly anyone saw him die	**Nemo fere** eum **morientem** vidit
Most of us think more of our own virtues than of those of our friends	Plerique **nostras pluris** quam **amicorum virtutes** æstimamus

* **Ullum** (Adj.) = *any* (*poet*), **quenquam** (Pron.) = *any man*. See MADVIG, Par. 90, 3.

I

He is the best painter in all Italy	Pictor est **qualis** in tota Italia **nemo**
A thousand soldiers	**Mille milites**
Ten thousand soldiers	Decem **millia militum**
Are you equal to bearing this great burden?	Num es **tanto** oneri **ferendo**? (Or, **par es**)
Anyone can boast that he is more learned than any one of his own pupils	**Cuilibet** promptum est gloriari se doctiorem esse quam **quemquam** e discipulis suis. (**Quemquam** by attraction, see Par. 63)
The hope of taking booty	Spes **capiendæ** prædæ
There were some that pitied the prisoners	Erant qui **captivorum** misererentur
You ought to have respected him as a father	Debuisti eum æque ac patrem **vereri**
I have a hundred horsemen and six hundred infantry	Sunt mihi cent**um** equites, pedites autem sexcent**i**
I expect the city will be captured	**Credo** urbem captum iri. (Or **vereor ne**, or **spero**, but not **expecto**)
I fear that something has happened amiss, and that some misfortune is troubling you	Vereor ne **quid** mali acciderit, ne **quod** infortunium te perturb**et**
The spirit, the purpose, and the feeling of a country are expressed in its laws	Animus et consilium et sententia civitatis in legibus **posita** est. (Verb, being Singular, agrees with nearest Subject)
He said that I was not wise, you say that I was not honest	Ille negavit me sapientem **esse**, tu autem negas me probum **fuisse**. (Note the Pres. Infin. after a Verb speaking in the Past)

MISCELLANEOUS IDIOMS.

He pities no one	**Nullius** (*not* **neminis**) misereretur
I have lost the book you gave me	Perdidi librum **quem** mihi dedisti, *or* **Quem** mihi dedisti librum **eum** perdidi
The quarrels of lovers should be treated as a renewal of love	Amantium iræ amoris integratio putanda **est**. (Or, change order, and write putandæ sunt amoris integratio)
My wife and son are dead	Uxor mea et filius **mortui** sunt
I will do it if I can	Hoc si **potero** (*not* possum) faciam
The general, in his usual forgetfulness, passed by the tents of the sentries	Imperator, ut erat mente immemori* (*not* e) vigil-**um** (*not* **ium**) tentoria præteriit
I yesterday asked him to come to Rome	Rogavi eum heri ut **Romam veniret**
The man that is freed from debt is void of care	Qui ære alieno liberatus est, is est **cura** vacuus
I am sorry to hear this	**Invitus** hæc audio
Many great disadvantages	Multa et magna incommoda
He will come with speed from Carthage	Carthagine **celerrime** (or **summa celeritate**, but not **celeritate**) veniet
For ten years he filled the office of a judge	Decem **annos** judicis munere fungebatur
I have asked him to come and see me to-morrow	Rogavi eum ut cras **veniat** me **visum**

* **Par** and **memor** always have **-i**; **pauper, princeps, superstes, compos**, always **-e**, and **dives** and **ales** generally **-e**. It would seem that those Adjectives that are used as Nouns, prefer the **-e**. The *Noun* **par** makes Abl. **pare**. So, use **sapiente** for the Noun, **sapienti** for the Adjective.

MISCELLANEOUS IDIOMS.

I will help you once and no more	**Semel**, non sæpius tibi subveniam
I am surprised at this	Hoc mihi admirationem movet. (Not **hoc miror**)
Sicily is opposite Carthage	Sicilia e **regione** est **Carthagini** (or **Carthaginis**)
I was once walking in a meadow	**Forte** in prato ambulabam
Why do you oppose me to no purpose?	Cur mihi frustra **adversaris?** (Not **opponis**)
I shall die and no one will help me	Moriar **nec quisquam** mihi succurret. (Not **et nemo**)
I shall abide by my opinion	**In** sententia **manebo**
Does anyone deny this?	Num **quis** hoc negat?
I cannot write for weeping	**Præ** lacrimis scribere non possum
Once a king reigned over Corinth	**Olim** (*or* **quondam**) rex Corintho præerat (**regno** *is Intransitive*)
I'll give all of you a denarius apiece	**Singulos** denarios **vobis** omnibus dabo
You are ten miles nearer the city than I am	**Decem** tu **millibus propius** quam ego, ab urbe **abes**
Trust as many men as possible	**Quam plurimis** crede
They will run on their several errands	Suum quisque iter **current**
He came to such a pitch of folly that he did not believe even his own father	**Eo stultitiæ** venit ut **ne** suo **quidem** patri crederet
One uses one medicine, another another	Alius alia medicina utitur
He came as soon as possible	Quam celerrime venit

MISCELLANEOUS IDIOMS.

Everyone trusts me, but no one will trust him	Omnes (not **quisque** nor **omnis**) mihi, nemo **autem** illi credit
He is more dutiful (pius) *than his brother*	**Magis** est quam frater, pius (not **piior**)
Everyone trusts me, but without any affection	Omnes mihi credunt **sed** sine ullo amore. (**Autem** adds something different, **sed** something limiting or contradictory)
I know you will grow cold	Scio **fore ut frigescas**
None of you will pardon me	Nemo **vestrum** (not **vestri**) **mihi** ignoscet
The country is ruined	Actum est de re-publica
There's no doubt, citizens, that he pities you	Non est dubium, cives, quin **vestri** (not **vestrum**) misereatur
The house is finished	Ædes **perfectæ** sunt (not **perficiuntur**: ædes sing. means *a temple*)
This will be a protection to me	Hoc erit **mihi** præsidio
I have warned you of this, and have left nothing undone that may be of use to you	**Hoc** te monui, **nec quidquam** prætermisi quod tibi utile esse possit
Some run one way, others another	**Alii alio** currunt
My name is Tullius	Nomen mihi est **Tullio** (or **Tullius**)
He died ten years after the founding of the city	Decem annis post urbem **conditam** obiit
The town had been surrounded by the enemy with a ditch	Hostis **oppido fossam** (*or* oppidum fossa) circumdederat

MISCELLANEOUS IDIOMS.

I sold for eightpence what I had bought for two shillings	Quod tribus denariis **emeram** id uno vendidi
He was condemned to death	**Capitis** damnatus est
Will you sell your life for two shillings a day?	Num **trinis** in diem **denariis** sanguinem vendes?
I do not mind being without riches	**Facile careo** divitiis
This was the man that deceived me	**Hic, hic inquam** me fefellit
I have ascertained that the fellow is wasting his time	**Compertum habeo** hominem tempus terere
The sun is many times larger than the earth	**Multis partibus** major est sol quam terra
He inflicted punishment on his (own) son	Filium suum **pœna** affecit
For ten years I have been a pupil of Socrates	**Decimum jam annum** Socratem audio
A peck of corn was at that time worth three sesterces	Tritici modius id temporis **ternis** sestertiis erat
You ought to have answered before	Antea **te mihi respondere oportuit** (or **debuisti mihi respondere**)
Troy was besieged by the Greeks for ten years	**Trojam decem annos Græci oppugnaverunt**
On our journey we were attacked by robbers	Latrones nos **ex itinere** adorti sunt
I prefer fighting on horseback to fighting on foot	Malo **ex equo** quam **pedes** (adj.) (or **pedibus**) pugnare
I think very highly of the excellent Tullius	Tullium, **virum optimum, plurimi** facio
He threw himself at the general's feet	**Imperatori** ad pedes se projecit

MISCELLANEOUS IDIOMS.

I heard him say that was not true	Audivi illum **negantem** id verum **esse**
You ought to have seen him jump	**Oportuit** te illum **saltantem** spectare
Why may I not be grave?	Cur mihi non licet esse **severo**?
Why did you build this great bridge over this small river?	Cur **in tam** parvo flumine pontem **tantum** fecisti?
It is possible you have made a mistake	**Fieri potest** ut errorem **feceris**
When we say "in Virgil," we do not necessarily mean "in the Æneid"	Si quando "**apud** Virgilium" dicimus, non continuo "**in** Æneide" dicere volumus
My dear friend Balbus is near the city	Balbus, **vir mihi amicissimus, prope ab** urbe abest
You and he promised to be present	Et tu et ille promis**istis** vos adfuturos esse
Trees flourish in the country, men in town	**Ruri** arbores, **in urbe** homines vigent
Horse, foot and baggage, all were destroyed	Equites, pedites, impedimenta, omnia periere (where "and" is to be omitted)
He blamed me without ascertaining what I had done	Me culpavit, **neque** quid fecissem intellexit
With his usual folly, the fellow denied it all, and that too in my presence	Homo, cujus est stultitiæ, omnia, **idque** me coram, infitiabatur
The enemy at once sounded a retreat. When he heard this, the general bade his men also retire	Hostes confestim receptui canunt. **Quod** quum audivisset imperator, **suis** quoque, ut recedant, imperat
With your usual kindness you will pardon his folly	Tu, **pro tua clementia**, homini stulto veniam dabis

As long as you are detained there you will never be free from annoyance	Quoad ibi **detineberis**, nunquam molestiis carebis
He died not long afterwards	Haud **ita multo post** obiit
You have more than four hundred horsemen with you	**Quadringentos equites amplius** tecum habes
They paid tribute once every ten years	**Decimo quōque anno** tributum pendebant
I propose to set out about ten in the morning	{Consilium est mihi / In animo habeo} **circiter** quartam horam proficisci
Anybody is believed by fools	**Cuilibet** (or **cuivis**) credunt stulti
As to the prisoners they are brought back, and no one has escaped	**Quod attinet ad captivos**, reducti sunt **nec quisquam** effugit
But no more of this, now I return to more serious matters	Sed **hæc hactenus:** nunc ad graviora redeo
He was alike treacherous in peace and in war	**Tam** in pace **quam** in bello infidus erat
He is two inches taller than any of his brothers	**Duabus unciis** procerior est quam **quisquam** ex fratribus
By the advice of Aristides they rejected the plan	Consilium, **auctore Aristide**, rejecerunt
No one but the consul heard him take the oath	Nemo **præter consulem** illum **jurantem** audivit
Boys are persuaded more easily than old men	**Pueris** facilius quam **senibus** persuadetur
He asked which was the younger of you	Rogavit **uter vestrum** minor esset natu
The man is good, but by no means wise	Vir est **ut** bonus **ita** nequaquam sapiens

MISCELLANEOUS IDIOMS.

I am on the point of giving battle to the enemy	**In eo sum ut** prælium cum hostibus **committam**
The two brothers exhorted one another	Fratres **alter alterum** hortantur
When did you hear that she sings?	**Quando** audivisti illam **canere?**
What town do you see yonder, pray?	Quod **tandem** oppidum **ibi** prospicis?
I am very intimate with the few friends I have	**Amicis** quos habeo paucos familiarissime utor
Everything that was of value was burned	**Quidquid** erat **pretiosi** concrematum est
One can scarcely avoid cold in one's house, much less in the open air	Vix in tectis frigus vitatur, **nedum sub divo**
He is a good, nay an excellent man	Vir est bonus, **immo potius** egregius
Every legion was divided into ten cohorts	**Omnes legiones** (or **legio quæque**) in **denas** cohortes divisæ sunt. (Not **omnis legio**)
Everyone hates ingratitude	Omnes **beneficii immemorem** oderunt. (Par. 3 *a*)
You are all but last	Minimum **abest** quin ultimus sis
I did not know whether he would not remain	Nesciebam **an** mansurus esset. (**Non** to be omitted)
Take care not to trust him	**Cave (ne) credas** homini
Next year he was returned by Cambridge for the second time	Proximo anno Cantabrigienses illum **iterum** delegerunt
Nothing is so narrow-minded and paltry as avarice	Nihil est tam **angusti animi** tamque **parvi** quam **amare** divitias

MISCELLANEOUS IDIOMS.

I could scarcely keep from venting my anger on him	Vix me continui **quin** iram in eum **evomerem**
I don't know whether you will do as I do	Nescio an **non** eadem atque ego **facturus sis**. (**Non** inserted)
Do you know when he will come?	Scisne **quando** venturus sit?
However wise he may be, he needs friends to help him	**Quamvis sit** sapiens, opus est illi amicis **qui** illi **subveniant**
Although I am absent, I like to hear what is going on at home	Quanquam **absum, libenter** tamen quid domi **fiat audio**
We were almost perishing	**Minimum abfuit quin** periremus
When I was recovering from my illness I was one day attacked by a bull	Quum ex morbo **convalescebam** forte taurus me **petiit**. (**Quum** temporal)
While this was happening the enemy fled	Dum hæc **geruntur** (pres.) hostes terga verterunt (perf.)
Whether this is true or false it does not at all trouble me	Hæc, sive vera **sunt** sive falsa, **nihil** (*or* **nullo modo**) me movent
When I approached the whelps the lion rushed at me	Quum ad catulos **accederem** leo me petiit. (**Quum** causal)
He asked me whether this was true or false	Interrogavit me **utrum** hæc vera **an** falsa essent
I perceived the kindness with which he received me	Intellexi **quanta** me benevolentia exciperet. (Not **benevolentiam qua**)
You have done well in coming here	Bene fecisti **quod** huc venisti

MISCELLANEOUS IDIOMS.

He answered he had sent the money to Lilybæum a few days ago	Respondit se **Lilybæum paucis abhinc diebus** argentum misisse
He died four years after he returned home	**Anno quarto** postquam domum **redierat** mortuus est. (N.B.—The pluperfect is allowed after **postquam** when the length of the interval is expressed)
I heard that the enemy had marched twenty miles by night and was now close at hand	Intellexi hostem viginti millia noctu progressum esse et **jam adesse**. (Not **nunc**, not **adfuisse**)
We accepted the terms on condition that the guards should be removed	**Ita** accepimus conditiones **ut** custodes removerentur
He is not a fit person for you to converse with	Non est aptus **quocum colloquaris**
He is too brave to fear death	**Fortior** est **quam qui** (*or* **quam ut**) mortem **timeat**
The soldiers were seized with fear that Cicero's wound might be fatal	**Pavor cepit milites** ne Ciceronis vulnus mortiferum esset
You are acting as foolishly as if you were questioning a deaf man	**Idem facis ac si** surdum interroges
Cæsar asked his soldiers why they distrusted their own valour or his energy	Cæsar ex militibus quæsivit cur de **sua** virtute aut de **ipsius** diligentia desperarent. (**Ipse** referring to the principal Subject, is used in contrast to **se** referred to a minor Subject)
We must wait till the elections are held two months hence	Expectandum est nobis **dum comitia** duobus abhinc mensibus **habeantur**

Socrates was called to trial on the charge of corrupting the youth, but in reality because he had become suspected by those in power	Socrates in judicium vocatus est quod **corrumperet** juventutem, **re tamen ipsa** quia in suspicionem magistratibus **venerat**
Instead of being true it is not even probable	**Tantum abest ut** hoc verum sit ut ne verisimile quidem sit
They grew alarmed that with his changeable and artful nature he might desert them and once more gain the favour of his countrymen	Pertimescebant ne, **homo vafer et inconstans**, ab **ipsis** descisceret et cum **suis** in gratiam rediret
Not till now did the citizens disperse to their homes	**Tum demum** cives suam quisque domum digressi sunt
If you help me I shall be rejoiced; if not, I shall not take it ill	Si mihi subvenies gaudebo; **sin minus,** haud ægre feram
Will you not inform me whether this is true or not?	Nonne me certiorem facies utrum hæc vera sint **annon**? (Or **necne**)
Nature prompts an infant to love itself	Natura movet infantem ut **se ipse** diligat. (**Ipse,** qualifying the Subject of a clause containing **se,** shews that **se** refers to the Subject of the clause, not to the principal Subject)
Suppose a man is selling a house because of some faults in it	**Vendat** vir ædes propter aliqua vitia
He said it wasn't like Greek manners for women to dine with men	Negavit **moris** esse Græcorum ut in convivio virorum mulieres accumberent (*or,* Acc. and Inf.)

MISCELLANEOUS IDIOMS.

The general encouraged his soldiers saying, "Why do you make useless lamentations? Press on. Why are we delaying here? Will not the enemy crush us while we delay? If you had obeyed me before, you would have been in safety by this time, and even now you may yet be safe. Be of good courage. Soon the cold will grow less severe."	Imperator milites in hunc modum hortatus est, "Cur inutiliter **plorarent**? **Instarent**! Cur ibi se morari? Nonne hostem se morantes oppress**urum** esse? Si sibi antea paruissent, illos jam in tuto **futuros fuisse**, salvos etiam tum esse posse. **Erigerent** animos. Mox **fore ut** frigus mitesc**eret**"
I have often seen my countrymen walking in the busy cities of Athens or Rome	Sæpe meos cives **Athenis** vel **Romæ, in urbibus** celeberrimis, ambulantes vidi
At one time he says this, at another, something else	**Modo** hoc, **modo** illud, dicit
The child hoped that the bird would grow tame	Puer (not **liber** except in pl.) speravit **fore ut avis mitesceret**
Panætius praises Africanus, giving as a reason that he was moderate	Panætius Africanum laudat quod **fuerit** abstinens
I prefer Alexander to Aristocles, not because the former is altogether wise, but because the latter is not wise at all	Alexandrum Aristocli antepono, **non** quod ille **sit omnino** sapiens, sed quia hic **est omnino non** sapiens. N.B.—**sit, est**
My father blamed me for not writing three letters to him in the whole of a year	Pater me culpavit quod per totum annum non **ad se trinas** literas misissem. (Note Distributive with **literæ, castra,** &c.)

Of males as many as 10,000 *were captured*	**Virile secus,** ad decem millia capta. (Used without alteration in apposition to all cases)
Zeuxis and Polygnotus did not use more than four colours	Zeuxis et Polygnotus non **plus quam quatuor coloribus** utebantur
Your advice is more honourable than expedient	Consilium das **magis** honestum quam utile (*or* honestius quam utilius)
He has perpetrated an almost unheard-of crime	**Tantum non** inauditum scelus patravit
Not less than thirty horsemen were killed	**Haud minus triginta equites** interfecti
All that survived the battle were taken the next day	**Si qui** prælio superfuerant capti sunt postridie. (Never **omnes qui**)
They set out for the bridge, which was fourteen miles off	Ad pontem—aberat autem millia quatuordecim—proficiscuntur
I am expected to remain	Omnes **confidunt** me mansurum esse (*or* **postulant ut**)
The general exhorted his men as follows: " Why do you make useless complaints? Press on"	Imperator milites hortatus " Cur ' **inquit** ' inutiliter ploratis? Instate!" (Note the introductory sentence left unfinished)
Don't despise a joke	Ne jocos **sis aspernatus** (not **asperneris**)
Who was there that did not hate you?	Quis erat **quin** te **odisset?**
We shall not be safe if Cicero is killed	Tuti non erimus si Cicero **occisus erit**
Some law were passed, others remained posted up	Leges aliæ latæ **sunt,** aliæ promulgatæ **fuerunt.** (Madv. 344)

MISCELLANEOUS IDIOMS.

How few there are that are prepared to die for their country!	**Quotusquisque est** qui paratus **sit** ad moriendum pro patria!
I asked him what o'clock it was, but he made me no reply	**Interroganti mihi quota hora esset** nihil respondit
What is the meaning of the word pleasure?	Quid vult vox **voluptatis?**
I can't hope it will be my good fortune to escape	Sperare non possum **fore ut contingat mihi** evadere. (Do not use fut. part. of compounds of **tango**)
He says that we shall not succeed if Cicero is killed	Negat **rem nobis bene successuram esse** si Cicero occisus **sit**. (Fut. changed to Subj. in dependent sentence)
I am writing this letter on the 7th of March, and I entreat you to answer as soon as possible	Has literas Nonis Martiis **scribebam** atque **oro** te ut quamprimum rescribas. (To the reader, the writing is *past*, the entreaty remains *present*)
Bid your friends collect with speed	Amicos tuos jube quam celerrime **convenire**. (Remember that **colligere** is Transitive)
After one or two days he called a meeting of all the surviving citizens	Post **unum et alterum diem** convocat **si qui** (*or* **quidquid**) civium supererant. (Or **qui cives ... omnes,** but not **omnes cives qui**)
What reason is there why your departure should be excused?	**Quid est causæ** cur abeas excusatus?
Suppose you were in my position?	**Fac**, quæso, qui ego sum esse te?

I wrote yesterday from Ephesus, to-day I write from Tralles	**Dederam Epheso** pridie, has **dedi** Trallibus
He is too rich to be in want of money	**Divitior** est quam ut pecuniæ egeat. (**Ditior** rare in prose)
See that you sell half-a-dozen houses	**Fac senas** ædes **vendas**. (Not **sex**)
I have no fault to find with old age	Nihil habeo **quod incusem senectutem**
It is said that Agesilaus lived to the age of seventy	**Dicitur Agesilaus** ad **septuagesimum annum** vitam egisse
You will do well to remember the difference between a friend and a flatterer	**Bene facies si memineris quantum inter** amicum et assentatorem **intersit**
Cuspius, from whom you will receive these two letters, is useful to me in many ways	Cuspius, a quo **binas** has litteras **accepisti**, multis in rebus mihi utilis est
After I had spent the month of May there, we were detained from the 3rd of June to the 12th September	Postquam ibi mensem Maium **consumpsi, ex ante diem tertium Nonas Junias usque ad pridie Idus Septembres** tenebamur
I shall not believe your promises, unless you fulfil what you have already promised	**Ita** credam promissis **si quæ** jam promisisti **solveris**
It was resolved to send ambassadors to ask what was the meaning of these repeated insults	Placuit legatos **mitti qui rogarent** quid vellent hæ tot **contumeliæ**
Yesterday evening he returned home to his family	**Heri, vesperi** domum ad **uxorem liberosque** rediit (not **familiam**)

MISCELLANEOUS IDIOMS.

With what decency, pray, can you insult thus so excellent a man as Tullius?	Quo tandem ore Tullium, **virum egregium tanta contumelia afficis?**
If he had not run away, I should have helped the poor man with pleasure	Homini miserrimo, **nisi aufugisset, libenter** (not læte, nor **voluptate**) **succurrissem**
I came to see you at once, inasmuch as I had received many kindnesses at your hands	Statim veni te **visum, ut qui** multa beneficia a te accepissem
This is too good to be true	**Meliora** hæc sunt **quam quæ possint** esse vera
You must be ignorant of your position	**Fieri non potest quin nescias** quo in loco sis. (Not **positum,** or **positionem**)
If I knew, I would tell	Si **scirem, dicerem** (I do not know, and my telling is impossible. Condition regarded as *impossible*)
But I should not have time, if I tried to relate it all	Sed tempus me **deficiat,** si omnia nunc narrare **velim.** (I might try, but I do not intend to. The condition is *possible*, but will not occur)
No one is so keen-sighted as not to be occasionally deceived	Nemo est **tam lynceus qui non** interdum fallatur
Would that you thought as I did, or, since that is impossible, would that you would think that I mean well	Utinam tu eadem atque ego **sentires,** vel, si hoc fieri non potest, utinam **credas** me bene velle. (Note various uses of *think*)

K

Cicero has been banished, a calamity that is deplored by every respectable person	Cicero ex urbe pulsus est, **id quod** (*or* **quam calamitatem**) boni plorant omnes
I shall leave nothing undone to banish the most turbulent citizens	Nihil prætermittam **quin violentissimum quemque** civium ex urbe pellam
He promised to come on the 11th of September, but did not come till the 11th of October	Adventum, quem **in ante diem tertium Idus Septembres** promisit, **in ante diem quintum** Idus Octobres distulit
What would you take to jump off this bridge?	Quid velis **mereri ut** de hoc ponte **desilias**?
It would have been better to have answered Yes or No	**Satius fuit aut Etiam aut Non** respondere
I asked him whether he would have helped me if he had been able	Interrogavi eum utrum mihi **subventurus fuisset** si potuisset
I praise this, not because it is honourable but because it is useful	Illud laudo, **non quod** honestum **sit** sed **quia** utile **est**
The enemy flock round in the hope of finding some inlet	Circumfunduntur hostes **si** quem aditum reperire **possint**
Instead of thanking me he abused me	**Quum** gratias mihi agere **deberet** mihi maledixit
In the case of a slave, this might have been maintained, not in the case of a free man	Hoc in servo **dici potuit, in** ingenuo non potuit
Alas for the deceitfulness of human hopes!	O **fallacem** hominum spem!
I am anxious for your sake	**Tuam vicem** sollicitus sum
I do not know what I should have done	Nescio quid **facturus fuerim**

GRADUATED EXERCISES.

(*Each Exercise is based on the one or more preceding exercises. For example, "your kind uncle Tullius," in the second Exercise, is an instance of the same rule as is exemplified in "the prodigal Balbus" in the first Exercise. The References in the first Exercises are to the Paragraphs in "Rules and Reasons."*)

HINTS FOR TRANSLATING CONTINUOUS PROSE.

1. Read over your English (*not one sentence at a time, but the whole passage*) till you have mastered its meaning.

2. Render abstract Nouns by simpler concrete Nouns, or by Periphrases, or by Phrases with Verbs. See Paragraphs 3, 3a.

3. Render English Metaphors by appropriate Latin Metaphors. See Paragraph 79.

4. In a group of English short coordinate sentences, find out which is the most important and make that the principal, and the rest subordinate. See Appendix, page 164.

5. Find out the connection between each subordinate part of a sentence and its principal part, whether it be cause, contrariety, sequence, consequence, &c. and use the appropriate links. See Appendix.

6. If there are any implied statements lurking in epithets, drag them out and express them by clauses with appropriate links. See Appendix.

7. Find out the connection of the first sentence with what (probably) preceded, and then of each of the other sentences with the sentence immediately preceding, and use the appropriate links. See Appendix.

INTRODUCTORY EXERCISES.

Exercise I.

1. It is said (5) that Cato was (a man) of upright character.
2. All of us, young and old, rich and poor, must die (5).
3. Foolish (persons) are easily persuaded (to) any thing (6).
4. We ought to believe good and honorable men (6).
5. If one does one's best (8), one ought not to be blamed.
6. No one of us is free from fault, but the better part of us (our nature) is divine (10).
7. Cæsar was on the point of (11) (**in eo esse ut**) taking the fort.
8. The good men were loved, the rich were envied (11).
9. While these things were going on (11) in France, Cæsar was waging war upon the Britons.
10. He did not let the enemy go till he had promised to observe the treaty in future (11).

Exercise II.

1. They may (possibly) come to us to-morrow (12).
2. Caius Julius! you might help me, if you would (12).
3. The enemy might return at any moment, and slay us all (12).
4. Would that my faithful friend knew the danger I am in! (12).
5. My friend! you should not do this (= ought not to).
6. Should they do this (12), they would deserve great blame.
7. They must all have perished (12), if the brave sailor had not promptly (**praesens**) helped them.

INTRODUCTORY EXERCISES. 133

8. You must come from England to Boston over the sea (12).
9. We must obey our parents, love our children, and fight for fatherland (12).
10. You must not (12) fancy that you are believed, (when) speaking falsely (participle).

EXERCISE III.

1. The boy is like his father (13) (in appearance), but the girl is like her mother (in disposition).
2. Cæsar ordered (**impero**) the soldiers to attack the wall, but the camp-followers he ordered (**jubeo**) to remain in the camp.
3. I am ashamed of my folly, repentant of my sins, and weary of life (13*a*).
4. It is our interest (13*a*) that our country should be prosperous.
5. He said it was his (own) interest to do-good to all men.
6. The herds are feeding-on rich pastures (13*a*), but the men eat various food.
7. The master teaches his pupils many (things), but the pupils conceal many (things) from the master (14).
8. He takes-away the life of his enemy, and tears off the arms from his body (15).
9. Terrified, the townsmen cast themselves at the feet of the conqueror (15, note).
10. The travellers set out from Boston for the country: they spent five days in the country, and then returned to the city (16).

EXERCISE IV.

1. My sister lives in the splendid house of her father-in-law, but I dwell in my own house (16, end).
2. Good children are (in the place of) a great joy to their parents (17).
3. The bold lion fiercely resists his enemies, but the timid deer flees quickly (18).

4. He besought his comrades not to desert him in this so great danger (19).
5. That brave commander, Alexander, and that wise philosopher, Socrates, were formerly greatly praised (19, note).
6. He said that Cæsar was not the man to yield to danger or death (21).
7. Cicero was the first to arise (21) in the Senate and accuse Catiline of dreadful crimes.
8. Tall trees are first struck by lightning (21, 22), and a tall tree is-blooming in my meadow (22).
9. No Christian (22) would-be-guilty-of (**admitto in se**) so foul a crime.
10. The braver a man is, the more merciful is he towards the weak (=every bravest man, &c., 22).

Exercise V.

1. Idleness is a very-degrading vice (23).
2. The horseman slew his embarrassed (**impeditus**) enemy with a sword (24).
3. Cicero upbraided Catiline with great bitterness (24).
4. In appearance he was a lover of his country, in reality a lover of himself (24).
5. In the judgment of all good men, he is convicted of base deceit (24).
6. We have been waiting at home for you, dear George, now many days (25).
7. The Gauls are said to have been naturally more impetuous than firm (25).
8. The King gave his faithful body-guard (**satelles**) a great reward for his so great services (27).
9. The exiled Emperor lived for several years in England, near London (27).
10. For the last twenty years, many wars have been carried on in Europe and America (27).

Exercise VI.

1. The city was taken in the fourth year after it had begun to be besieged (28).
2. Trees and flowers bloom in summer, but decay and wither in winter (28).
3. What is the price of wheat in the market to-day? Seven dollars (29).
4. The good citizen values money and magistracies highly, but virtue and integrity more highly (29).
5. The saucy boy snapped his fingers and said, "I don't care a straw for you" (29).
6. The King of the Cappadocians, (while) rich in slaves, was without money (31).
7. Relying on (32) the valor of his army, Louis (**Ludovicus**) Napoleon waged war on Germany.
8. The boy was born in high station, and is descended from noble ancestors (32).
9. Desire of glory and wealth are great incitements to undergoing (gerundive) dangers (33).
10. A good general has need of valor, of prudence, of great experience in warfare (33).

Exercise VII.

1. The harbor of Boston (adj.) is capable-of-holding (34) many war-ships and merchant-vessels (**navis oneraria**).
2. The wise-man is no less firm of purpose than capable-of-restraining (=powerful-over) evil desires (34).
3. Cicero was unjustly-accused of tyranny and cruelty, but Catiline was justly condemned for treason and parricide (36).
4. It-is-the-characteristic-of a prudent-man to deliberate carefully about important matters, and of a foolish-man to act rashly (38).
5. This State is bounded on the east and south by the Atlantic Ocean (39).

6. William Evarts, the illustrious lawyer, departing from his home at Boston, fixed his abode at New York (**Eboracum-novum**) (39).
7. The Germans attacked the army of Cæsar in front and rear on its march (39).
8. The rest of the Carthaginian ships were taken in the 607th year after the foundation of the city (40).
9. Before the Birth of Christ, many wonderful portents appeared (40).
10. The traveller arose by night, and about nightfall arrived at home (41).

Exercise VIII.

(For this and the fifteen following Exercises, refer to 41, The Prepositions).

1. Do not try to do any thing beyond your strength.
2. The brave leader and above three hundred soldiers were lately slain by the Indians.
3. My friend, strive to be above deceit.
4. According to Thucydides, the Athenians managed their affairs ill.
5. The good and the bad will each be rewarded according to their deeds.
6. Immediately after his consulship, Cicero set out for his country-house.
7. After your letter, mine was immediately read.
8. After the manner of bandits, they plundered all things, public and private.
9. We ought all to live agreeably to nature.
10. The orator speaks as agreeably as possible to the truth.

Exercise IX.

1. We justly esteem cowardice among the basest vices.
2. The battle of Cannae (adj.) was memorable **amongst** Roman defeats.

INTRODUCTORY EXERCISES. 137

3. He was the only young man among many who won for himself fame.
4. The victorious general divided all the booty among his men (**sui**).
5. The city, taken by storm, was at the mercy of the conquerors.
6. At the beginning of the battle, the enemy were courageous and elated; at the end, they were cast down and dispirited.
7. Is your dear daughter at the point of death?
8. The beautiful lady held a looking-glass before her
9. Fifty tried warriors were on guard before the Prætorian gate.
10. Through the whole of life, death and disease present themselves before the eyes of mortals.

Exercise X.

1. Verres was brought to trial before the jury, at the instance of Cicero (= Cicero being accuser).
2. The captive Gaul boldly made (**habeo**) a speech before the general.
3. Sulla died nineteen years before the Consulship of Cicero.
4. The slanderer is beneath the notice of honorable-men.
5. What you say, my dear son, is beside the mark.
6. The heavy rains had caused the river to swell beyond its bounds.
7. That so good a man should utter-falsehoods is beyond belief.
8. The city prætor will, beyond question, be brought to trial for extortion.
9. The Sabines, making an onset, all but took the city.
10. What else is the history of a nation, but the history of men?

Exercise XI.

1. Mæcenas had a splendid country-seat by the Anio.
2. When the messengers arrived, my sons and daughters were sitting by me.
3. My son came to Boston by sea, but the journey is now generally performed by land.
4. As often as she was by herself, the widow bitterly mourned for her dead husband.
5. The robber committed the robbery by himself.
6. Our friend will set out for London on the 1st of May, and will return home by the 15th of October.
7. Cæsar was informed by spies that the Helvetii had set out from home with all their forces.
8. Some ancient writers said that Ireland was less by a half than Britain.
9. By Heaven! I implore you, do not commit so great a crime!
10. By what you say, the last hope is now lost to us.

Exercise XII.

1. The Helvetians thought their territories too small, considering their numbers.
2. During four years, he used to call upon me twice or thrice a month.
3. During the night, my uncle saw a terrible dream.
4. During the reign of Charles I., the great English Rebellion occurred.
5. During the reign of George III., the American Provinces gained their liberty.
6. We are delighted with our house, except that it is not large enough.
7. While I was dwelling in the country for two years, I sent no letter except to you.
8. All bitterly abused me, with the exception of one, or, at most, two.

INTRODUCTORY EXERCISES. 139

9. Exclusive of his personal property, the wealthy merchant has left his wife large estates.
10. Exclusive of many vices, Catiline, according to Sallust, was guilty of foul crimes.

EXERCISE XIII.

1. The barbarians of the Southern (**australis**) Islands used small shells for money.
2. The fanciful-man (says Horace) exchanges round-buildings for square.
3. Let us fight bravely for our wives, for our children, for our fatherland!
4. I fear greatly for you, my son, but not at all for myself.
5. For Heaven's sake (= by the gods I beseech you) come quickly and help me!
6. The dishonest judge took bribes for deciding a suit contrary to evidence.
7. He had been chosen for the magistracy, which had been appointed for the following year.
8. It is my intention to set out for Rome on the 20th of August.
9. I will wait for a longer time even than you have asked for.
10. Out of many such deeds, this one will perhaps serve for an example.

EXERCISE XIV.

1. For my part, I intend to go to the country at the beginning of next summer.
2. The soldiers in the camp are suffering severely for want of provisions.
3. As for the physician whom you mention in your letter, I know nothing about him.
4. For success that youth is both too trifling and too idle!
5. Take courage, worthy (excellent) friend: there is no cause for despair!
6. For all I know, the excellent poet has perished at sea.

7. Be assured you are no match for that strong and active wrestler.
8. So much for that matter! Now let us turn our thoughts to other things.
9. It were better for many guilty-men to escape (avoid) punishment, than for one innocent-man to be condemned to death.
10. He writes with such care that it is rare for him to make even a single blot.

Exercise XV.

1. From his boyhood, he was eagerly-desirous of learning.
2. From the time when I returned home from England, I have suffered severely with tooth-ache and head-ache.
3. From (being) poor, our friend has suddenly become rich.
4. From Romulus's name (says the legend) the city was named Rome.
5. The French nation now is different from what it once was, under the great Emperor.
6. Messengers came from Carthage to Hannibal to warn him not to return home.
7. The German monarch wrested his kingdom from the Emperor of the Franks.
8. Rest from labor and care comes only to the dead.
9. He generally comes into the city to buy supplies once in seven days.
10. Both in Herodotus and in Homer we find many incredible tales.

Exercise XVI.

1. The Great Desert of Sahara extends about nine hundred miles in width, and three thousand in length.
2. The orator exhorted the assembly in this manner for more than two hours.
3. Paul, the famous Apostle, was born at Tarsus, was put in prison at Philippi, and suffered death at Rome.

INTRODUCTORY EXERCISES. 141

4. In my judgment, said Clearchus, the traitor deserves to be put to death.
5. If we wish to live in accordance with Nature, we must live in the country.
6. In addition to this, he had great patience and wonderful fortitude.
7. In case of your father's death, what will you children do?
8. In comparison with those dwelling in hotter countries, we deserve to be considered happy.
9. In consequence of the defeat at Cannæ, great fear came upon the Romans.
10. Catiline was going in the direction of Gaul, when Q. Metellus Celer met him.

Exercise XVII.

1. His liberality, skill in warfare, and good-fortune were in favor of Caius Cæsar.
2. It is said that the Emperor wishes to abdicate in favor of his son.
3. In the midst of the enemy, many of whom he had slain with his own hand, lay the leader stabbed with a sword.
4. The eloquent senator spoke long and vehemently in opposition to the proposal.
5. In point of numbers the Swiss nation is weak, but in point of valor it is very strong.
6. Americans spare no toil in the search-after riches.
7. Your son is not deficient either in respect of natural-ability or in knowledge.
8. In spite of all the brave citizens could do, the city was taken by assault.
9. In spite of the intercession of many powerful men, the murderer was hanged on the gallows.
10. Pythias was instead of a brother to Damon, and they were mutually willing to die, each for his friend.

Exercise XVIII.

1. Scotland is on the north-east of Ireland.
2. The enemies' army is within ten miles of the city.
3. The active father said to his idle son, "This comes of laziness."
4. To come of good parentage ought to be a stimulus to good deeds.
5. They found in the camp many vessels of gold and silver. (*Turn two ways.*)
6. There are many men of ability, but only few of great ability.
7. Very few of us now survive who remember the famous general.
8. The Battle of Cannae was near (did not want much of) bringing destruction to the City of Rome.
9. Rooks build their nests in the tops of trees.
10. Before rain, leaves and feathers float on the surface of the water.

Exercise XIX.

1. He ordered the captain not to stir a finger's breadth from that-spot (**illinc**).
2. Many persons, shut in by snow in the midst of the mountains, perished of hunger.
3. News of the death of the general and his brave soldiers was first brought by an Indian scout.
4. I greatly desire to ascertain what has become of my classmate, who went many years ago to India
5. What think you of the measures which have recently been brought before the Senate?
6. Huntsmen and warriors ought to be swift of foot, ready of wit, keen of eye, and bold of hand.
7. In the year 479 B.C., a great-sea-battle between the Greeks and Persians took place off Mycale.
8. Many tombs of illustrious men are still standing on the Appian Road.

INTRODUCTORY EXERCISES. 143

9. Sardanapalus, as he rushed-forth to meet the enemy, had a wreath on his head, and a sword in his right-hand.
10. Vienna (**Vindobona**) is on the Danube, 340 miles from Berlin (**Berolinum**).

Exercise XX.

1. On the north, Spain is bounded by the Pyrenees Mountains, on the west by the Atlantic Ocean.
2. Cæsar and Ariovistus held a conference on horseback.
3. We heard the poet playing skilfully on the lyre.
4. The Spartan soldier was carried home to his mother on his own shield.
5. When Darius was on the point of death, he wished both of his sons to come to him.
6. The Senators were mostly on Pompey's side, the common-people on Cæsar's, and many cautious men were on neither side.
7. On the side of the Helvetii, the mountain gradually slopes down to the plain.
8. My friend excuses himself from coming to my house on the plea of health.
9. Bad men obey the laws, not willingly, but out of fear.
10. Boys often inflict injury, not on purpose, but out of fun.

Exercise XXI.

1. The famine in Egypt lasted many years (over many).
2. Hannibal the Carthaginian, (while) very young, was set over the army.
3. The Isle of Man is over against Britain on the west.
4. It was owing to the rashness of Lentulus to a great extent (**magnopere**) that Catiline's Conspiracy did not succeed.
5. Pending the giving of judgment, the defendant had committed suicide.
6. Themistocles persuaded his countrymen (**civis**) to build a broad and high wall round Athens.

7. The Sabines sent ambassadors round to the neighboring States to excite them to war against the treacherous Romans.
8. Ever since America won her freedom (**se in libertatem vindicare**), she has been increasing in riches, fame, and power.
9. Never since the creation of the world have arts flourished more than in the present day (= these times).
10. It was chiefly through his wealth that Tarquinius Priscus rose to be King of Rome.

Exercise XXII.

1. My friend will set out from Boston on the 1st of August, and will go first to Italy, then to Smyrna, and lastly to the Crimæa.
2. The German Empire extends from the Baltic Sea to the shores of the Adriatic.
3. Our soldiers fought with the Indians to a late hour in the day, when they were overwhelmed by superior numbers (**multitudo**) of enemies.
4. Having slain many of the enemy, the small band of American soldiers was slain to a man.
5. To what end do you utter so many-words, which have no bearing on (**nihil pertinens**) the subject.
6. The orator mounting the rostra, whence he had so often before harangued the people, spoke to this effect.
7. To be dutiful to (one's) parents, loyal to (one's) fatherland, faithful to friends, firm towards foes are (the characteristics) of a good citizen.
8. To the best of his power Hector defended Troy against the attacks of the Greeks.
9. The cavalry, under Philip's command (*abl. abs.*), charged suddenly towards the hills which look toward the east.
10. Achilles felt towards Patroclus the love of a brother, and therefore exacted heavy vengeance for his death (= him slain).

Exercise XXIII.

1. Under the pretence of reconciling the alienated friends, by treacherous calumnies he rendered them more hostile to each other.
2. The Servians under arms have invaded the Turkish (Turcicus) territories, and have fought some battles with poor success (**male gerere**).
3. Under the appearance of a favor, he inflicted on his client a severe injury (= affected his client with).
4. The Jews were continually fighting with one another, when they ought to have been fighting against the Romans.
5. Having the wind with him, the merchant sailed quickly from Boston to Dublin (**Eblana**).
6. I will do at once what you request, with all my heart.
7. The decision of the suit rests-entirely with the chief judge
8. With heaven's aid, we may (**licet**) hope to overcome all enemies, and surmount all dangers.
9. Cicero, with his usual wisdom, defended both the city and himself against the desperate (**perditus**) conspirators.
10. The boy fell into the river and was within a very little of being drowned.

Exercise XXIV.

1. Without (75) attempting to conciliate (45) even his friends, he (2) succeeded in conciliating even his enemies.

2. There is no doubt that (54) all the magistrates in the (16 end) populous city (40) of Antioch (64), (2) conspired to dethrone the (18) just king Tullius.

3. What reason have you (page 94) for saying that the (18) foolish young Balbus will not return (16) to Corinth?

4. I am (6) persuaded that you are wrong and (45) nothing shall persuade me (page 89) to believe otherwise.

5. I will help you if I (par. 11, page 8) can, but I fear your friends will (49) not help you, and, if (70) so, there is no doubt (49) that you (49) will be banished.

6. (51) Whether this is true or false, it does not persuade me (page 89) to believe that (18) the excellent Balbus is guilty.

7. I will ask him (51) whether he (64) wished to remain at (16) Carthage, or to set out for (16) Rome.

8. He says the bird will never (page 98) grow tame (**mitesco**), as long as it (11) is kept in a cage.

9. I fear (49) (64) he wished to converse with (page 56) me.

10. There is no doubt (49) that he (64) promised to come to (16) Athens, (44a) but he did not perform (53) what he promised.

11. The (18) sagacious husbandman said the weather (**dies**, pl.) would (page 98) grow cold (**frigesco**).

12. I (2) expect that (51) whether he comes to Rome or remains at Naples he will not be (2) secure. Nothing (hint* 7 and appendix) but his (3a) departure from Italy will satisfy me. ('Turn by **ita ... si discesserit**: see page 49.)

13. After the (18) thoughtless Tullius (11) had asked me (page 89) to dine with (page 56) him, he (page 88) promised to dine with Balbus in the same day.

The reference is to the hints on page 131.

14. Did not you read the (19) two (**binas**) long, interesting letters (**literæ**) (54 end) that my good friend Tullius sent me ten days (page 35) before his death?

15. The hot-tempered (11) captain (hint 4 and appendix) perceived (21) the treachery that was intended, (47) and answered (page 43) in haste, (Oratio Recta, 78) "Do not (12) send messengers to these (19) blood-thirsty people. (Hint 7 and appendix.) The citizens have sworn to admit nobody. (Hint 7 and appendix.) of you (12) will send some one, don't send anyone you have a liking for. Send a bachelor."

---

1. I fear the prodigal (18) Balbus will die within a week. If so, all (54) that he has will be sold, and (45) nothing will be left to support his child. But the man has no cause (75) for finding fault with anyone but himself; for, after (*postquam*) he had (66) squandered his father's patrimony, instead of (75) working (24) with vigour, he left his family (2) at Rome (16) without (41) money to (73) buy them bread, while (67) he travelled from Rome to (16) Milan, and from Milan to Paris, begging from (7) anyone that he met on (39) the way. I have often entreated him to (73) improve, but all in vain.

2. What reason had you for finding fault in this way with your kind and considerate uncle Tullius? He did his best to help you, and would have done more, if you had not refused to obey him. I fear that in ten months' time you will repent, when too late, of your disgraceful ingratitude; meantime I entreat you to remember your promise to improve. You have not much time to fulfil your promise, for he writes to me that, when he arrives at Naples, he intends to sell his estate there and to return to Rome with speed. (75, 70, 49, page 89, 11, 16.)

3. There is no doubt that if he pities us, he will be a great protection to us in these sad calamities; and indeed the town

has now been surrounded by the enemy with a ditch, so that I fully expect that it will be captured in ten days from this time. If our spies had warned us of this before the enemy came to Naples, we should have been able to resist them with some chance of success; but, as it is, I fear that we shall be captured or put to death to a man. One thing I wish to know before you go, viz. on what day the general promised to send a messenger to the town of Nola. (11, 12, 2, 64, 16.)

4. The excellent Balbus, when in his old age, while studying Greek at Corinth, used to say that "he was afraid he should not succeed, like Cato, in learning a new language, for his memory failed him and his old energy had gone." And indeed, although some one in Cicero says that he has no fault to find with old age, we certainly must not expect to retain all the vigour of youth. So do not promise to perform when old, what you have neglected when young. I have often asked how old Balbus was when he began Greek; but I could never ascertain his exact age. But I believe he was over seventy. (18, 70, 2, page 98, 12, 54, 64.)

5. Although my kind friend Tullius promised to help me, he forgot his promise. The consequence was that (*ut*) I was left, while a boy, at Rome, without money to take me home; and there was no one to help me in my sore distress. Indeed, if the worthy Balbus had not seen and pitied me, I do not know what I should have done. His enemies used to say that he loved no one, and that no one loved him; but he asked me to come home with him, and treated me all the time I was in his house, like a man of humanity, as he was, with kindness and consideration. (76, 18, 70, 73, 45, page 77, 60, 24.)

6. I don't know whether there is anything more agreeable than to hear one's praises uttered by some one who is free from flattery. The following remark of Cicero illustrates this better than a thousand treatises on flattery:—"The most subtle flattery," says that author, "is to tell your friend that he is above flattery, and to say that you do not know how to flatter him." It happened once that a Roman senator, named Lentulus, had a needy obsequious Greek fellow dining with him, who tried in vain to flatter his host. Lentulus laughed at his awkward attempts, and said, (*Orat. Rect.*) "I flatter myself, sir, that I am indifferent to flattery." (*Orat. Rect.*) "Had I known that," replied the Greek, "I should have known how

to flatter you, but you have taught me a good lesson, and I will not forget it." (8, 25, 12, 46.)

7. Almost all the men in the ship, when they saw nothing but rocks and waves before them, thinking that the boat was not fit for use, flung themselves into the sea and swam towards different parts of the beach. But all to a man perished. Only the sailors in the boat managed to escape to the shore. When they had reached it, they asked the natives to grant them food, clothing, and shelter: for they had nothing, not even a morsel of bread, to satisfy their hunger. But, instead of friends, they found robbers drawn up to meet them on the beach: they were then deprived even of the little clothing they had, some of them were beaten, some of them threatened with death, one was killed. In this extreme misery they were met by a band of three thousand soldiers coming from the capital, which was ten miles off. The commander of this force received them with kindness, asked them whether they wished to go on to the capital or to return at once to their country; and, upon their deciding on the former alternative, ordered that each should receive ten pounds (*Orat. Rect.* and *Orat. Obl.*). "What more," he added, "can I do for you? Only say and it shall be done."

8. In these great calamities, the brave and intrepid general, instead of manifesting fear, turned to his dejected soldiers and said, (*Orat. Obl.*), "Courage! all will be well! We shall succeed past expectation, if we do our best to teach the enemy that they can be resisted by brave men. Why do we delay here in idle conversation when we ought to be up and doing? I am informed that 20,000 infantry, 4,000 cavalry, and fifteen ships of war have been despatched against us; but do not fear them, for, while they are mercenaries, we are free men. The enemy will certainly not pity you, and there is no hope but in arms."

9. On the receipt of this sad news, the two generals, with joyful looks intended to disguise their feelings, began to ask their guide how much stronger the enemy was than their own army. On hearing that the Athenians had 3,000 more infantry than they had, one of them turned to the other and said (*Orat. Rect.* and *Orat. Obl.*), "It is all over with these exultant soldiers of ours, if, instead of retiring, we march forward to Athens. You see, by these two letters in my hand, that our largest army

was yesterday defeated, almost all that survived were captured, and no one but the consul returned to tell the tale. Though the Athenians are treacherous enemies, they have no lack of bravery, and I fear that, if we do not retreat, we shall repent." After hearing these words, the other general asked for time to deliberate before making up his mind what ought to be done.

10. The celebrated Caius was once asked whether the man that believed nobody, or the man that believed everybody, was the wiser. He answered, that every virtue was a mean between two vices ; that it was possible for us to believe too much, as well as to believe too little (*Orat. Obl.*). "Cannot anyone see that it is the duty of a wise man to distinguish between those that are worthy, and those that are unworthy of credit? for it is, and always will be, a part of virtue not merely to desire to do right, but also to determine what is right." While the wise Caius was saying this, his pupils listened with attention. After he had finished, some of them remained behind to ask him the meaning of what he said ; others said that there was no truth in it ; others left without saying a single word themselves, or thinking in the slightest degree about what had been said by their teacher.

11. In the war with the Germans, this cruel and arbitrary king, being desirous of making, in the night-time, some alterations in his camp, ordered that, under pain of death, neither fire nor candle should be burning in the tents after a certain hour. He went round the camp himself, to see that his orders were obeyed: and as he passed by Captain Tullius' tent, he perceived a light. He entered, and saw the captain seal a letter, which he had just finished writing to his wife, whom he tenderly loved. (*Orat. Obl.*) "What are you doing there?" said the king. "Do not you know the orders?" Tullius threw himself at his feet, and begged for mercy, but he had no power, and made no attempt, to deny his fault. (*Orat. Rect.*) "Sit down," said the king to him, "and add a few words that I shall dictate." The officer obeyed, and the king dictated, (*Orat. Obl.*) "To-morrow I shall perish on the scaffold." Tullius wrote it, and he was executed the next day.

12. Amid the shouting of the soldiers the voice of the general was distinctly heard as he encouraged those who were advancing to the charge, and rebuked the fugitives (*Orat. Obl.*). "Why," he cried, "are you retreating? Do you hope to find safety in

flight? Do you not know that even the timid deer does not always flee? On the one side lies the sea; and on the other the enemy. Death is on both sides of you—choose between a death of honour and a death of shame. If even now you do not fight for your country, it is all over with the glory of Rome." On hearing these words, all the best of the soldiers recovered their spirits, closed their ranks, and charged the enemy with fierceness. The latter, unprepared for this sudden attack, fled some in one direction, some in another; none were spared, and not a man out of that vast multitude was left to carry back home the news of the sad result.

13. To this the general answered that he could not help recollecting the great cruelty with which his soldiers had been treated by the enemy at the taking of Nola, seven years ago (*Orat. Obl.*). "Now," he said, "nothing but compassion prevents me from destroying all of you to a man. You have not enough food to satisfy you, not enough even to keep off famine. Whether you are assisted by the Romans or not, it matters little; all of you must perish." Upon this, the ambassadors, bursting into tears, promised that their countrymen should give all they had to the soldiers if only their lives were spared. They did not say that they had not deserved death; for if they had said so, it would have been of little use: but they flung themselves at the general's feet, and again and again begged for pardon. He heard them in silence, without raising them, or appearing in any way to be touched by their calamities.

14. (*Orat. Obl.*) "If," said the wise shepherd, "you had observed the weather, as you promised to do, and had not forgotten the instructions I gave, you would not have come into this painful position. When, about a couple of weeks ago, an inundation took place, all the shepherds that were in the neighbourhood collected in haste and came to me for advice. On receiving my advice, they thanked me for the pains I had taken, and assured me they would carry out all that I had recommended. Consequently, although another storm visited us in the following week, scarcely anyone was injured, and I do not believe that you will lose a single sheep for the future, if you will adopt the same course as they did. Instead of weeping, give up your folly. Why did you come here but to get advice? and why are we sent into the world but **to battle with troubles like these?**"

15. When the renowned Balbus, who had conquered Persia, Tartary, and Syria, was defeated by Tullius, and taken prisoner, he sat on the ground, and a soldier prepared a coarse meal to appease his hunger. As this was boiling in one of the pots used for the food of the horses, a dog put his head into it, but, from the mouth of the vessel being too small, he could not draw it out again, and ran away with both the pot and the meat. The captive monarch burst into a fit of laughter : and, on one of his guards demanding what cause upon earth could induce a person in his situation to laugh, he replied (*Orat. Obl.*), "It was but this morning the steward of my household complained, that three hundred camels were not enough to carry my kitchen furniture ; now it is carried with ease by that dog, who hath carried away both my cooking instruments and dinner."

16. On hearing this, the passionate queen replied in a fury (*Orat. Rect.*), "I am surprised that I have not persuaded you that the course I recommended is the best under the circumstances, and I regret that you seem to have forgotten the great kindnesses you have received from me and from my predecessors on the throne." Then, growing more and more angry as she proceeded (*Orat. Obl.*) "For what purpose," cried she, "have we marched here but to fight the enemy? Do you wish to give up your rights and liberties to the detestable Balbus? Although I cannot dictate to you the course you should follow, I entreat you to listen to me when I appeal to you, in the name of the national honour, not to desert me in this degrading position. Why did you promise to obey me, if you did not intend to keep your word? What have you asked of me that you have not obtained? Prepare, I beseech you, to conquer or to die. If I had known that you wished to surrender the city, I would never have come on this disgraceful journey."

17. (*Orat. Obl.*) "Can I ever fail," said the grateful Tullius, "to recollect the favours I have received at your hands? Depend upon it, I will do my best to deserve success, even though I cannot attain it ; and you shall have no cause to regret the kindness you showed me in my many severe troubles. But why do I delay when I am called elsewhere by duty. Farewell!" The wise old judge replied as follows:—(*Orat. Rect.*) "I am indeed glad to hear what you say, and nothing will make me believe that you are ungrateful. I advise you and your friends, instead of trying any longer to conciliate Balbus, to collect together at once and oppose him. I am sure he will never be persuaded by mere

argument, and if he is not put down in a few months, you will be seriously injured by him."

18. As the agents of the infamous queen were conducting her unfortunate husband to the strong castle, ten miles off, at Cumæ, the scene of his tragic and sorrowful end, it came into their minds that to prevent his being recognized by the people on the road, it would be well to have his head and beard shaved. They accordingly commanded the prince to alight from his horse, obliging him to sit down on a mound by the wayside; meanwhile one of the escort, who officiated as barber, brought a basin of cold water taken out of the next ditch, observing to the king that "for that time any water must do." The prince, deeply affected, burst into a flood of warm tears, and seeing them fall into the basin, he pathetically observed (*Orat. Obl.*), "Behold, monsters, nature supplies what you would deny."

19. On hearing this the impetuous soldier, with his sword drawn, rushed into the midst of his rebellious comrades, and cried at the top of his voice (*Orat. Obl.*), "Why do we stay here in this narrow camp, waiting for the enemy to crush us? Why do we continue to obey an incapable general? Did not you thank me for the bravery I showed in representing your claims to the general? And did you not promise to join me? Collect then at once, and in haste. Seize the officers. Instead of delaying, adopt the same course as our comrades in France ten days ago adopted, and you will have no cause to regret the result. Success is certain if you but do your best. Are you not ashamed of the disgraceful position in which you have been placed for more than a fortnight?" Here he paused for a moment, and then added, with bitterness (*Orat. Rect.*), "Perhaps some one will say we must not forget the oath of fidelity we have sworn to our generals. We will not forget it, on condition they remember the duty of kindness towards us."

20. In the midst of all these terrible disasters the brave general was the only man that retained his presence of mind. Collecting a few of the most resolute men in the army, he reported them to act with energy, and not to forget the great glory that awaited them if they could only force their way through the enemy and reach a place of security (*Orat. Obl.*). "Why," said he, "do you despair, when I am your leader? Has the enemy any reason to boast of having ever defeated me? It is not

the enemy that I fear, it is your timidity and irresolution. Before you came to Naples you acted with the courage of soldiers; now, you are in some strange way altered, and I do not know what is the matter with you; if you had marched with speed, you would now be in Rome, and not a man there would dare to oppose you."

21. Remembering the cruelty with which their countrymen had been treated by the enemy, the ambassadors came most unwillingly on their humiliating errand, and, after they had arrived at the capital and obtained an audience in the town-hall, no one liked to be the first to speak. At last the excellent Tullius broke silence with these words (*Orat. Obl.*):—"Although we cannot expect indulgence, and do not ask you to pity us, yet we think it worth while to appeal to your sense of your own interest, and to ask you to give us time to consult our government as to whether we may surrender the city. Remember that it is sometimes profitable to spare the vanquished, and that mercy is sometimes the mark of a politic as well as of a merciful man. The oldest of your nobles cannot have entirely forgotten the great calamities that befel you in the late war. What you have suffered once it is possible, if not probable, that you may suffer again. However, if we cannot persuade you that our advice is the best, we are prepared to resist you to the last."

22. (*Orat. Obl.*) "I was not so much injured by the wound," cried the intrepid soldier; "it was the man's treachery in attempting to stab me when off my guard that provoked and angered me. I thank you with all my heart for the great kindness you have shown me while ill, and now farewell. Believe me, I shall not find it easy to forget the many benefits you have bestowed on me in my severe trial. Why do not all men remember, as you do, the claims of hospitality and mercy? Can I ever repay you for your trouble? Never, except by imitating your conduct. Before I knew you, I was persuaded that every Roman was a knave; now I know that wherever I go I shall find in all nations some goodness, kindness, and compassion: and nothing shall make me believe the contrary."

23. At the unfortunate battle of Damietta against the Saracens, Louis IX. was taken prisoner. He bore this reverse of fortune so nobly and so magnanimously that his enemies said to him in admiration (*Orat. Rect.*), "We look upon you as our captive and

our slave; but though in chains, you behave to us as if we were your prisoners." The sultan having sent one of his generals to the king, to demand a very considerable sum of money for his ransom, his majesty replied, (*Orat. Obl.*) "Return, and tell your master, that a King of France is not to be redeemed with money: I will give him the sum he asks for my subjects that are taken prisoners; and I will deliver up to him the city of Damietta for my own person." And such were the terms on which the liberation of the King of France and his subjects was afterwards effected.

24. A thousand promises cannot restore the reputation forfeited by one dishonourable act, and it ought never to be forgotten that a readiness to make professions and promises often implies a readiness to break them. But, while we cannot help distrusting a man that seems to promise much and feel little, we ought to be on our guard against suspecting a man unduly. We ought to be wise, without being cruel or suspicious. A man of good feeling will do well to remember that he, as well as others, is liable to go wrong, and the precept that enjoins upon us not to judge lest we be judged will be always in his mind. If we remember this solemn precept, we shall be more likely to act not only with mercy but also with wisdom in our relations to our inferiors, and there can be no doubt that, in spite of apparent failure, gentleness will in the end succeed where cruelty will fail.

25. (*Orat. Rect.*) "Do you dare to say," cried the infuriated mutineers, "that the soldiers in the camp did not again and again entreat you to lead them against the enemy? Have you anything to reply to this accusation? If so, speak: if not, confess that you deserve death." To these words the general replied (*Orat. Obl.*), "I see that you are determined to murder me Yet my oldest lieutenant will bear me witness that I shewed my prudence in giving orders for a retreat. I had only 2,000 men at that time with me. I did not know which of the two roads through the wood led to Rome. Upon my proposing a retreat to my officers, they all kept silence except two, who expressed their approval of it; and, in the end, it was unanimously determined on. As for the prisoners, it is true that none were spared; but the reason was that several tried to escape after they had promised not to depart from the camp. What more could anyone have done in that great calamity? I for my part do not know, and I wish my accusers would each produce his own plan."

26. After inquiring why the principal men of wealth and importance in the town did not interfere to prevent these great tumults, Tullius unfortunately turned to the general Fabius and said (*Orat. Rect.*), "I am surprised that your country has not obtained more wisdom from its misfortunes. You asked me just now what we should have done if we had been conquered. I reply, we should at least have learned moderation." On hearing this, the general was filled with anger and replied (*Orat. Obl.*), "Why do you make such absurd remarks? Can I or anyone avoid destiny? What is the use of talking about what might have happened? It serves no purpose but that of irritating the people. Cease to waste time in this way and depart from Rome with speed, taking your goods with you. If you do not, I promise to accuse you of treachery in three days, and you and thousands of spies like you shall be put to death." Tullius was persuaded that he meant what he said, and he therefore collected his goods, bade farewell to his family, and, after asking them to write to him as soon as possible, set out in haste for Egeria, a town about twenty-five miles distant.

27. The wise and pious philosopher, turning to the rash and foolish youth, replied with calmness (*Orat. Rect.*), "If, while young, you do not pay attention to your work, you will find, when old, that you will have cause to repent your folly. There are many that are admired, while young, for their quickness, ingenuity, and taste, and, if they had determined to work with steadiness, they would have succeeded; but, instead of doing so, they often waste their time in an idle and frivolous manner, and thus they are left far behind in the race of life by others of inferior ability but greater application." To this the young man replied in haste (*Orat. Obl.*), "I have a great dislike to receive such lectures from you; and there is no reason why you should select me instead of others, since others are as bad. Pray cease, if you don't wish me to leave the room. I shall go home to my friends in Italy at once. Can anything be more absurd than that a youth of ability like mine should continue to remain at school?"

28. It was customary with General Caius, when any of his soldiers were brought before him for heinous offences, to say to them, "Brother, you or I will certainly be hanged;" which was a sufficient denunciation of their fate. Once a spy, who was discovered in his camp, was addressed in this language. Next day, as the poor wretch was about to be led to the gallows, he pressed earnestly to speak with the general, alleging that he had somewhat of importance to communicate. The general, being made acquainted with his request, said with roughness (*Orat. Obl.*), "It is always the way with these rascals; they pretend some frivolous story, merely to reprieve themselves for a few moments: however, bring the dog hither." When he was introduced, the general asked him what he had to say. (*Orat. Rect.*) "Why, my lord," said the culprit, "when I first had the honour of your conversation, you were pleased to say that either you or I should be hanged; now I am come to know whether it is your pleasure to be so, because, if *you* won't, I must; that's all." The general was so pleased with the fellow's humour that he ordered him to be released.

29. In this great perplexity I had recourse to the active, energetic Tullius, one of my most intimate and affectionate friends. I took him by the hand, informed him of the difficulty in which I was placed, and asked him to advise me what to do, and, if possible, to assist me with money. He answered, with his usual kindness, "If you had asked me to help you on the 23rd of March I would have done so with pleasure, but now, instead of being able to help you, I want help myself. It is true that a few days ago I possessed friends, money, and arms; but now I have not even food enough to last me and my children for seven days. Can you hope for help from me after hearing this?" While he said this, the tears ran down his face. I felt the sorrow with which he was moved, and there was not a man present that did not feel it as much as I did. For my part, I turned away my face so as not to shew my feelings, and I told Tullius that I would only consent to take the command of the army on condition that he had his property restored to him.

30. I once heard a Frenchman and a German arguing together as to which was the better country; the former spoke of the successes in war that had been obtained by his nation, and enumerated the distinguished generals that had gained conquests innumerable. The German reminded the Frenchman of the discoveries in art and science that had been effected by his countrymen; the beauty of their literature, the world-wide renown of their poets, their historians, and their philosophers. While they were thus arguing together, it happened that an Englishman came up, who put in a claim for his own country in the following words (*Orat. Obl.*) :—"Although we admit that

the French have more taste, and the Germans have more depth than our own countrymen, yet still in practical ability we think that we are not inferior to any nation : for answer this question —What nation has succeeded like ours in administering its affairs at once in peace and prosperity ?"

31. (*Orat. Rect.*) "If," said the philosopher, in answer to the question of his brave young son, "if, in our great calamities, we had been spared by the conquering Romans, perhaps we should have pitied them in turn. But, instead of pitying us, they treated us with cruelty on all occasions ; I am therefore much surprised at your regretting the rapidity with which the army of Carthage, under the leadership of Hannibal, conquered the armies of Rome." Seeing that his son kept silence, the old man went on as follows (*Orat. Obl.*):—" For my part, I am as happy to see the defeat of Rome, as the Romans were to see that of Spain fifteen years ago ; and I am sure, if you remember the past history of our nation, that you will feel it to be your duty to do everything you can to procure the defeat of the Romans and the success of the Carthaginians. If you agree with me, I am satisfied ; if not, I will endeavour to prove, by narrating the history of the past war, that ambition, pride, avarice, and cruelty, must inevitably be the ruin of any nation, and that Rome can form no exception to this rule."

32. The angry and passionate queen, resenting the insult she had received from all the wealthiest inhabitants of the city, replied with bitterness (*Orat. Obl.*), "The most exalted genius is frequently overborne by envy. I am determined to do everything that I can to effect the ruin of this rebellious people, for I am certain that their wants will never be satisfied, and that until their wants are satisfied they will never cease rebelling. They would persuade me, forsooth, that the sovereign is made for the nation, instead of the nation being made for the sovereign ; they complain that I neglect public merit, and lavish the revenue of the state upon unworthy favourites, and that all the most important offices are bestowed by favour. For my part, instead of being moved to pity by such complaints as these, I shall collect my most faithful troops in haste ; I will then surround the city, arrest the ringleaders, banish some, fine others, kill others, and thus establish peace."

33. It is said that even this hard and cruel tyrant was touched with gratitude at the haste with which the poor lame cobbler had

come to his assistance. After he had remarked that the favourites of kings were often the most deserving men in a country, he proceeded to describe the rebellion and the measures that had been taken to put it down (*Orat. Rect.*). "If," he said, "my generals, instead of sparing the people, had destroyed all the forests in the country, broken down the bridges and burned the villages, we should in all probability have succeeded, and we should not now be obliged to ask for peace. We should not have before us the spectacle of a city so vast and beautiful as this, besieged on all sides by enemies whom it is impossible to resist, and equally impossible to persuade to peace." Then, turning to the bystanders, who displayed much emotion at his words, he said (*Orat. Obl.*), "Leave me; why do you delay? Make the best of your way to the nearest refuge, for there is nothing to prevent the enemy from at any time taking the city; and, while I value your sympathy, I do not feel justified in endangering your safety."

34. I cannot be persuaded that you have done wisely in not visiting the castle. It is a place worthy of being seen for its own sake, and I hardly think that any is more strongly fortified both by nature and art; and to those who have read the chronicles of England it is rendered more memorable by a beautiful instance of filial piety. Two hundred years ago, the town was besieged and greatly straitened for want of provisions. No one could be found bold enough to undertake the dangerous task of conveying supplies thither, until a youth, whose father was in the garrison, came forward and accepted the duty. For several nights he crossed the lake, climbed the wall, and placed provisions at a spot where his father would find them. At length he was taken prisoner and sentenced to death, to strike terror into anyone who might be disposed to render similar help to the besieged. It was the good fortune of one of my own ancestors to obtain pardon for him. With considerable danger to himself, he procured an interview with the general, and addressed him pretty nearly as follows:—"Affection to a father is the source of patriotism. You cannot put the youth to death without also causing pain to every good son." Not to make a long tale, he succeeded in his prayer, and the youth was spared. For my part, ever since I heard this story, I have always felt proud of my ancestor's conduct, and never think of the old castle but with feelings of interest and pleasure.

35. During the wars in Flanders, in the reign of Queen Anne, when the Duke of Marlborough and Prince Eugene commanded the allied army, a soldier, in the division of the latter, was condemned to be hanged for marauding. The man happened to be a favourite with his officers; they therefore applied to the Duke of Marlborough, begging his grace to interfere. With his usual good nature, he accordingly went to Prince Eugene, who said (*Orat. Obl.*) he never did, and never would, consent to the pardon of a marauder. (*Orat. Rect.*) "Why," said the duke, "at this rate, we shall hang half the army; I pardon a great many." (*Orat. Obl.*) "That," replied the prince, "is the reason that so much mischief is done by your people, and that so many suffer for it; I never pardon any, and therefore there are very few to be punished in my army." The duke still urged his request; on which the prince said (*Orat. Obl.*), "Grant me this favour. Make inquiry which of us has executed most men, and if your grace has not executed more than I have done, I will consent to the pardon of this fellow." The proper inquiries were accordingly made, and it appeared that the duke had executed far more than Prince Eugene, on which he said to the duke (*Orat. Rect.*), "There, my lord, you see what example can do. You pardon many, and therefore you are forced to execute many; I never pardon one, therefore few dare to offend, and of course but few suffer."

36. After Tullius had heard that the brave young soldier Balbus had returned to the town of Tarentia, forty miles distant, he went and visited him to see whether he was contented with his position in the army, and to ascertain how matters were going on in the camp. He was delayed for a day or two by the illness of an intimate friend, but three days after Balbus' return, Tullius arrived at Naples and called on Balbus. On seeing him, he addressed the young soldier thus (*Orat. Obl.*):—"However much, my dear Balbus, I am gratified by the report of your many illustrious achievements, yet I feel that as long as you are in the army, your conduct can never entirely meet with my approval. For what, after all, is a soldier? He is a man that will cut anyone's throat for a shilling a day." Hereupon the impetuous Balbus replied in haste (*Orat. Obl.*), "Why do you talk like this? Pray cease. Do you not know that a soldier may sometimes be one of the most deserving men in the country? Besides, whether your observations are true or false, they are sure to be useless, as long as human nature remains as it is."

37. "We should not have taken these harsh measures," said the ferocious old general, "against all the most respectable citizens in Rome, if we had not known for certain that the people in Rome will never be quiet, and will never submit to our dominion in peace." He then continued to speak as follows :—" Even all the brilliant successes of our army have been unable to convince the Italians that resistance is impossible, and that it is absolutely necessary for them to come to terms. There will always be found cruel generals and undisciplined and disobedient soldiers, and I confess that, although we have done our best to avoid injuring private individuals, yet the life of the agriculturists in Italy during the past four months has been by no means an enviable one. But did you not know when you went to war the risk you were incurring? And did not we take up arms to improve our condition if possible? Cease, then, from unavailing complaints."

38. (*Orat. Rect.*) "Look at my withered body," said the camel to Jupiter. "Why have you not given me the plumpness of the horse, the ox, and the elephant? Why have you given me so few muscles, and made me so ugly? And why have you compelled me to dwell in a dry, barren, and flat country like Arabia?" To these complaints Jupiter answered with a smile (*Orat. Obl.*), "My excellent friend, you will find that I have a reason for all I have done. If I have made you lean and deprived you of all superfluous muscles and flesh, it is because in the dry barren deserts of Arabia it is not possible to obtain much food. Why else did I give you this powerful jaw-bone except that you might chew the hardest nutriment? For the same reason I gave you a small stomach to prevent your eating too much. And as for my obliging you to live in Arabia, how, with your fat, fleshy feet, could you ascend the heights of mountains, or walk without slipping in the mud of marshy districts? Instead of talking any more nonsense, be kind enough to return to your work."

39. (*Orat. Obl.*) " If the matter is neglected longer," said the wise Tullius, "the country will not be safe. We ought not to hesitate in this great calamity to choose a general to meet the enemy before they arrive at Rome; and nobody, I think, will deny that we ought not to have hesitated when the Carthaginians were first collecting their forces. For when they were at the river, not more than ten miles off, would it not have been easy for us, even with a small number of men, to repel a regular

army? We have lost an opportunity; but now, without delaying longer, let us collect with speed our bravest citizens, and before the enemy advances further I hope to crush him with ease." When they heard this, the soldiers shouted for joy; declared to a man that they would have Scipio for their general; crossed the bridge with speed; marched for three days through a waste district called Gergovia; met the enemy suddenly near the Anio, and completely defeated them.

40. When Field Marshal Balbus was taken prisoner at the battle of Corioli, a Numidian hussar, who seized him, perceiving that he had a valuable ring, said, "Give me your ring." The marshal instantly complied with the demand of the captor. A short time after, when he was liberated by General Tullius, and the Numidian hussar had become a prisoner in his turn, he with great unconcern drew the marshal's ring from his finger, and presenting it to him said (*Orat. Obl.*), "Since fate has turned against me, take back this ring; it belonged to you, and it would not be so well to let others strip me of it." Pleased with the honesty of the hussar, the marshal bade him keep the ring in remembrance of his having once had its owner for his prisoner.

41. Without attending to the arguments of the merciful officer, the ferocious and passionate general replied (*Orat. Rect.*), "Whether you are speaking the truth or not, what you say has no effect upon me, and I never asked you whether it was your desire to spare the lives of the citizens of Corioli, a city that has done us as much harm as it possibly could. What I asked was, how soon it could be taken, for there is no doubt it will be taken sooner than people think. Now, instead of giving me advice, I order you, as I ordered you ten days ago, to collect all your bravest soldiers and to prepare for immediate action." On hearing this, the young man replied (*Orat. Obl.*), "If I have spoken freely, it is because I am persuaded that unless you do your best to conciliate the men of Corioli, and unless you promise to send them back all the hostages they have given us, not merely will you lose the hope of success, but the very safety of the army will be in danger. You may blame yourself for your present misfortunes, for you might have managed matters very differently. If you had taken the advice I gave you, you would not now be in this great difficulty. Every town in Italy would favour you, and not a man would wish to oppose your progress. I know of my own knowledge, that 300 of the bravest men of Naples determined to help you on condition you did not storm Corioli."

42. (*Orat. Obl.*) "I may well complain of the neglect with which I have been treated by my best friends," cried the proud and passionate queen. "I have no one to help me, no one to advise me what to do in this great calamity. Instead of coming to this dangerous place I might have travelled with ease to the city of Athens, which is not more than thirty-two miles off, and if I had done so I should have escaped my cruel enemies, and now I should be in safety." On hearing this, the aged Tullius, the wisest of her nobility, said (*Orat. Obl.*), "Why does your majesty complain? For these last two years you have been desiring nothing so much as an opportunity for engaging with the enemy—a desire that is now on the point of being gratified. Now, therefore, that the opportunity has arrived, why do you delay to avail yourself of it? Why does the army remain here inactive? I ask your pardon for speaking with freedom, but if your majesty does not communicate to the officers the exact time at which you will fight to-morrow, and the army is not prepared for an immediate conflict, the mercenaries, with their usual fickleness, will desert your standard, and you cannot possibly hope to succeed."

43. (*Orat. Rect.*) "I wish you would tell me," said the wise philosopher to the young man, "what is a worthy object to pursue through life." (*Orat. Obl.*) "The first thing," said the young man, "that I should like to do, would be to succeed in business; then, after amassing a considerable fortune, I should like to rise till I had become one of the principal persons in my neighbourhood; then there are all sorts of prospects that would be open for me. With a little tact, and the judicious expenditure of a little money, I could get into parliament; and when a man is once in parliament, there is no limit to the career before him." (*Orat. Rect.*) "But what do you expect to do in parliament?" said the philosopher. (*Orat. Rect.*) "I should endeavour to create a sensation," replied the young man. (*Orat. Obl.*) "But do not you think," said the philosopher, "that such an object as this is unworthy of a really noble man? Instead of endeavouring to make a sensation, had you not better find out what work you are best fitted to do, and do that as well as you can? Believe me, the highest object of a human being is to make the world a little better for his having lived, and not to make a sensation."

44. When the Samnites under their brave king Tullius defeated the Etrurians in the battle of Cumæ, the King of Etruria, seeing

his troops flee, asked what was the number of the Samnites who were making all this slaughter? He was told that it was only King Tullius and his men, and that they were all on foot. (*Orat. Rect.*) "Then," said the crafty Etrurian, "God forbid that such a noble fellow as King Tullius should march on foot," and sent him a noble charger. The messenger took it and said, (*Orat. Obl.*) "Sire, the King of Etruria sends you this charger, that you may not be on foot. Be pleased to accept it as a token of his respect." The brave Tullius was as cunning as his enemy, and ordered one of his squires to mount the horse in order to try him. The squire obeyed: but the horse proved a fiery one, and the squire being unable to hold him in, he set off at full speed to the pavilion of the King of Etruria. The king expected he had caught King Tullius, and was not a little mortified to discover his mistake.

45. After he had with patience heard the rash young soldier make his defence, the general addressed him in severe tones as follows (*Orat. Obl.*):—"I feared some time ago that I had made a mistake in sending you to take the command of the forces in Rome, and now I know for certain that you are not yet fit for the command of a large army; I shall therefore order you to return to your home ten days hence. You have pleaded that your intentions were good; but that is not the question. There is no one but believes in the rectitude of your intentions, and thinks you honest and well-meaning; but however well-meaning one may be, a man is not fit (to) for command without self-control, tact, judgment, and energy; and these qualities you do not possess." The young man in sorrow replied (*Orat. Rect.*), "I have nothing more to say in self-defence; I feel that I no longer deserve your confidence; and though I am conscious that I meant well, yet I must admit that I ought not to have left the city against orders. If I had known my defects sooner, I should not have asked you to appoint me a general."

46. (*Orat. Rect.*) "Away with these compliments," said the grateful Balbus; "the attachment between us is too great for it to be right, either that you should offer me thanks for any attention, or I you. I have not paid you an attention, I have repaid it. I think that I have received acknowledgment enough indeed, if what I have taken real pains to do be acceptable to you. There is no reason why you should thank me, if for your numerous uncommon kindnesses towards myself I have repaid you with this trifling service. So far from deserving praise, I should

have deserved to be considered most ungrateful if I had failed my friend. Whatever I possess, whatever can be done by my pains, reckon as much your own as your own property. I think that I have received a benefit in the kind construction you have put upon my services. If you heartily approve my services, mind you make a more frequent use of them. I shall not believe that you are pleased with what I have done, unless, whenever you want anything of mine, you take whatever you like, instead of asking for it."

47. Amid a profound silence, the renowned and eloquent Tullius arose and spoke as follows (*Orat. Obl.*) :—" Why do we delay? Is the crafty and cruel Balbus delaying? Do we not know for certain that he is making it his object to betray his country? Beware of regarding your private interests and disregarding the interests of the public. If you delay, it is all over with the state; either Rome or Balbus must fall: choose which shall perish." The senate heard the orator with admiration, adopted his opinion, and decreed that the consuls should provide for the safety of the country. On receiving this intelligence, the conspirators, in fear and trembling, betook themselves with all diligence to their respective homes, and none dared to utter so much as a word in opposition. They fled in different directions, some to Sicily, some to Athens; poor old Cathegus, now an old man of seventy-three, was the only one left at Rome.

48. (*Orat. Rect.*) "There is no doubt," said the ferocious general, "that all that have been taken with arms in their hands will be banished; for indeed it will be the height of folly, if men, who without any prospect of success rebel against their king, are spared, and allowed to go unpunished." To this the wise and merciful king replied with gentleness, but at the same time with firmness (*Orat. Obl.*), "There is certainly a great deal in what you say, and I recognize the zeal with which you have espoused my cause; but remember that because a man pities the innocent, it does not necessarily follow that he is weak-minded. Indeed, oppression is as impolitic as it is cruel. Why, then, do we delay to throw open the prisons, and to allow all the best of the prisoners to return with speed to Rome, especially as they have not bread enough for the people there? I, for my part, will take care of the destruction of the bridge that spans the Tiber, and I hope that in a few days, by surrounding the city with a wall, we shall make the rebels see that their position is untenable, and we shall induce them to lay down their arms.'

49. Tullius, turning with a look of contempt to Balbus, addressed him in these words (*Orat. Rect.*) :—" I do not know what reason there is why you should think you may keep your own property, and use that of other persons. There never was any reason why you should think so. What would you have thought, if a man had violently entered your house, beaten your servants, insulted your family, taken your money and all your valuables, and refused to make satisfaction? But this is just what you have done. I ask you then with what decency you can attempt to excuse such conduct. Actions like these have made you so hated that there is not a man in your neighbourhood but would be delighted to hear of your death. Indeed, you have so alienated all, that even your friends without exception desert you. A man must be a villain indeed to be deserted by his friends, and not to have a single person to take his part. Where is your old reputation for spirit and courage which you had when a youth? If you had a spark of courage, you would not bear such ignominy with tameness." On hearing this, the wretched Balbus, spite of his ordinary impudence, was touched with remorse. He went home, told his servant he was ill, shut himself up in his bedroom, made his will, took out of a chest a good stout rope, fixed a nail in the wall, fastened the rope to the nail, and hung himself—thus endeavouring to heal a life of error by one last fatal error.

50. When the Gauls under the command of Brennus had got possession of Placentia, they carried their cruelty to their Italian prisoners to the severest extremities, making them work like horses at their mills, and in drawing water. The acute and learned Balbus, in his travels, relates that he met some of these unfortunate wretches on his first entrance into the city, who had been liberated that morning from their dungeon, and who were endeavouring literally to crawl to the village of Alma, which was but ten miles off. (*Orat. Obl.*) "The legs of these poor creatures were swollen to a size that was truly horrible, and their eyes were terrible from inflammation. Some, too weak to support themselves, had fallen on the sand, where they were exposed to the scorching beams of the sun. Immediately on seeing Balbus and his companions, they uttered such moans as might have pierced the hearts of their cruel oppressors. They begged for water, but the travellers had none to give them : and all they could do was to prevail on one or two of the men of Alma to promise to take care of them until relief could be obtained. Of these unfortunate

captives, upwards of forty perished every day from the miseries to which their conquerors exposed them."

51. The industrious and acute philosopher turned with calmness to the rash young man and said (*Orat. Obl.*), "I am surprised at your acting with such thoughtlessness and want of good feeling; you have occupied now for ten years an honourable position in the estimation of all Rome, and you would now give up this position. Instead of paying attention to the duties of your office, you propose to bury yourself in a life of contemplation, and to desert your family. If ten days ago your best friends had known of your intention, and the haste with which you intended to leave them, they would all to a man have expressed to you the sorrow with which they received your determination. Give up then this hasty, thoughtless plan; your friends will be delighted to receive you home. Did you not hear yesterday that your most faithful servants were seeking you everywhere?"

52. This great and illustrious general would soon have obtained all the help he wanted from his countrymen, and would have driven the enemy out of the country in disgrace, had he not been prevented by the arrival of his great adversary Tullius. As soon as the latter reached the camp he began to sow discontent among all the bravest soldiers. He went first to one, then to another, and endeavoured to persuade them to mutiny by such words as these (*Orat. Obl.*):—"Do you know that your general means to betray you into the hands of the enemy upon the first opportunity? If not, why is the camp placed in this disadvantageous position? Why are we wasting our time instead of marching upon the undefended city of Nuceria, barely ten miles away? Rouse up your courage, and depend upon it that, if you are prepared to resist the commands of your general, I shall be ready to put myself at your head and to take upon myself the responsibility of leading you in this terrible crisis. Once this would have been difficult. Now nothing prevents you obtaining your rights once for all."

53. The general made answer as follows (*Orat. Obl.*):—"The enemy that you have been so long seeking is now only two miles distant: prepare then to conquer or to die. I will send spies to bring me word of their numbers and the position of their camp; this done, I must entrust the rest to you. Remember that your country depends upon you. If you conquer, you will enjoy ease, plenty, freedom, and glory; if you are defeated, you will

experience the only treatment you will deserve, that of slaves: up then and quit yourselves like men. Ten days ago you were eagerly longing for a battle : do you now shrink back? Ask yourselves whether you prefer a glorious death or an inglorious flight." At these words the soldiers were filled with fury ; they cast aside fear, they forgot their complaints, and promised one another to conquer or to die : and there was not one who thought victory for a moment doubtful. Soon afterwards all retired to their several tents, and there, by the command of the general, rested themselves till night brought darkness and the conflict. The general then ordered all the bravest centurions to appear before him, for the purpose of receiving their several instructions.

54. After the general had cast round his eyes, and had examined each rank in turn, he turned to the place where all the bravest officers were assembled, and said (*Orat. Rect.*): "Send some one at once to tell the king that I have examined the soldiers, and that no one here is guilty." After these words he turned towards the soldiers. He was ashamed of them, he said (*Orat. Obl.*); he could scarcely believe them capable of such gross ingratitude and cowardice. Why had they arms in their hands but to fight against the enemies of their country? "Why," he added, "do we delay here, as though we did not purpose battle. Away with such shameful cowardice! (*Orat. Obl.* still.) If you fight bravely, I promise you 16*l*. a-piece ; if not, you shall be decimated, and no Englishman will assert that I have acted with harshness towards you. Ten days ago you were all clamouring for battle ; why do you now decline it? When in the city you cried for war ; now that you are in the camp do you cry for peace?" Although the general had not been at the head of his army more than three months, the soldiers had learned to respect him. He was only thirty-two years old, but in this great peril he displayed the sagacity of age with the courage of youth. Though therefore he addressed them with bitterness and with reproaches, they listened to him in silence, instead of threatening him as they had threatened their former commander.

55. The inhabitants of this island were so bold that they would have preferred a thousand deaths to disgrace if the choice had been necessary. One brave farmer was asked why he would sooner die nobly on the field of battle than live ignobly at home. He answered (*Orat. Rect.*), " Because I am more afraid of shame

than of death." It happened once that they were invaded by the powerful nation of the Ventidii, who landed on their shores, marched up to their capital, devastated the country all round, and then laid siege to the city. The citizens determined to resist with boldness. Instead of throwing themselves at their enemies' feet, they sent away their families, their old men, and their treasures, and prepared to resist with desperation. Though they were prevented by scruples from committing suicide, they promised one another to fight so desperately that the enemy should not take them alive. When they were all assembled in arms, their general addressed them thus (*Orat. Rect.* and *Obl.*) :—" Remember, citizens, that victory or death awaits you. I will say no more; the enemy is at the gates: what reason is there for delaying?"

56. The despairing husbandmen, looking at the rising flood, exhorted one another to patience, and the eldest of them all, turning to his fearful companions said (*Orat. Rect.*), " Be of good cheer! There are not less than 300 of us. Yesterday I sent a messenger to ask for help; to-day I have sent another to report our perilous condition. I am persuaded that our houses, if destroyed, will easily be repaired, and we shall recover all the cattle that survive the deluge." Then, hearing a few of them murmur, he continued thus (*Orat. Obl.*) :—" We must do our best not to disgrace our reputation, for indeed we are in such a terrible position that we need all our faculties. What help is there except in industry and courage? Nothing but God and our right hands can rescue us from destruction. I am now old, and very different from what I was when a boy; but I will use all the strength I have in the task of assisting the wretched, and I am persuaded that there is not one of you that will not do the same. I hoped, indeed, that the waters would have diminished five days ago; but, though you are disappointed, remember that you are Englishmen, and, whether the waters rise or fall, behave as Englishmen should. To work! why do we wait longer?"

57. The citizens at first stood by in silence, and all the most respectable of them manifested, by the expression of their countenance, the sorrow they felt. At last the eldest of their number, on hearing of the taking of the city, after asking her majesty to allow him to speak, stepped forward and addressed the queen as follows (*Orat. Obl.*) :—" Your majesty has asked us what cause we have to complain, and has declared that as long as

discontent prevails in our country prosperity will not increase. Suffer us, however, to remind you that your generals, without even hearing what we have to say in our defence, have razed four of our best towns, and are even now butchering 300 men a day. The meekest and mildest will turn upon an enemy that threatens their race with extinction; already there are rumours of rebellion; these rumours will soon increase, and rebellion will commence. We should have resisted this cruelty before now, if we had been able, and we are sure that if your majesty does not as soon as possible command these cruel generals to desist, you will soon not have one faithful subject in the country. Pardon our freedom. Is it not much better that we should say what we feel than that your Majesty's empire should be endangered?"

58. On hearing this, the brave but rash general replied in anger (*Orat. Obl.*) :—" Soldiers! I am surprised at your cowardice; and I did not think that the men whom I have been commanding for twenty years would have deserted me in this emergency. Is there any hope of success except in bravery? Did you not promise when you swore fidelity to me nine years ago, soon after the capture of the two camps near Naples, that you would always obey the slightest intimation of my wishes? Away! You are no longer worthy to be my soldiers, nor am I coward enough to be a fit general for you and the like of you." At these words, the most respectable of the soldiers were much grieved. After a short deliberation they sent the brave captain Tullius to the general, and he spoke briefly to this effect (*Orat. Rect.*) : that the whole army were determined to obey the general, with the exception of one or two mutineers, whom they would select and hand over to the general for execution.

59. The brave soldier continued his narrative amid the attention of all present (*Orat. Rect.*) :—" On leaving Naples the enemy proceeded with 600 of their bravest horsemen, and 10,000 infantry, to Nola, a town that is at no very great distance from Naples, and is a convenient station for troops. Here they committed all sorts of atrocities; they slew some two and tortured others, arrested all the most wealthy citizens, burnt down the principal buildings, and destroyed the bridge; finally they marched out, leaving the place a ruin. And if our forces had not arrived in time to save Præneste, that town also would have suffered the same fate." (*Orat. Obl.*) "Indeed," continued the soldier with earnestness, "this is the most cruel war that I ever

heard of; the conquered are not spared on either side, and the bravest soldiers are hardened by war till they take pleasure in cruelty. You, my friends, are happy in never having experienced the horrors of war; do your best, then, to keep them at a distance from your shores, and do not grudge a few thousand pounds for this purpose."

60. (*Orat. Rect.*) "With all his faults," said the kind-hearted soldier, weeping, "our general was brave, just, and merciful, and there was no one that did not trust him." Then, turning to his fellow-soldiers, who were assembled in great numbers to ask for their pay, he said (*Orat. Obl.*), "Cease from thus execrating the memory of the dead; have you forgotten the many occasions on which our general led us to victory? Can you not remember the many brilliant distinctions we gained under his command? Did we ever prefer a reasonable request to him that he would not grant? But this is just what you always do—you curse to-day the man whom you will bless to-morrow." This was what the brave captain Tullius said, and if the other soldiers had been like him, the rebellion would have been quelled, and the city of Naples, with all its fortifications and supplies, would not have been surrendered to the enemy in such haste. But, instead of listening to him, the infuriated soldiers selected the most turbulent of their number they could find, and, under their leadership, marched in haste to Rome.

61. (*Orat. Rect.*) "You will have no chance of attaining the truth," said the wise philosopher to the young and thoughtless Tullius, "unless you bestow more patience upon the investigation of truth;" then, seeing the young man preparing to interrupt him without allowing him to finish his sentence, he said (*Orat. Obl.*), "Suffer me to finish what I am saying. Have you persuaded yourself that you are seriously studying, while you are merely taking up from time to time any subject that attracts your attention and learning a smattering of it? Did I not endeavour to persuade you to study some one science with thoroughness and steadiness? And did I not propose to give you all the assistance I could, if you liked to study the history of your nation and your national literature? Without knowing something of the history of one's nation, it is impossible for a man to be a gentleman, much less a successful politician. And I will further beg you to consider the extent to which a desultory course of study and the acquisition of a smattering of many subjects tends to

make a man conceited, frivolous, and idle, if not positively immoral."

62. The angry and sorrowful queen scarcely knew in this great calamity which alternative to prefer, whether it was better to give up her empire, or to run the risk of being killed. However, with her usual firmness, she soon decided on the fit course to pursue. Sending for the sergeant of her body-guard, she informed him of all that had occurred, and requested him to send the ten strongest men that he had, armed and prepared for a journey to Rome (*Orat. Obl.*), "Meanwhile," she said, "I shall remain here; and though I am now an object of pity, the time will come when I shall be admired by my friends and dreaded by my foes, and there will be no one who will maintain that the queen of Rome did not behave with courage and with wisdom." After she had spoken thus, she left the palace with the intention of quitting the city. But so great was the fury of the crowd, consequent on the queen's refusal to appoint her successor, that from sunrise to sunset they beset the city gates, demanding a change of ministers and the execution of the unfortunate courtier whom the queen had chosen last for her principal adviser—a request which they well knew the queen would never grant, even though her refusal might cost her her own blood and that of all her most faithful soldiers.

63. On finding that his friends were in this great misfortune, the wise and prudent philosopher turned to the rash young Tullius and advised him as follows (*Orat. Obl.*):—"If you had only listened to the advice I gave you ten years ago, you would not have been brought into this great peril, and you would not have been forced to seek safety by such disgraceful means. What has been done, however, cannot be undone. Why, therefore, do you delay longer here? Did not your wise mother, when she sent money to you at Rome not very long ago, send a friend at the same time to inform you of the pleasure with which she had heard that your life was spared, and of her willingness to receive you home whenever you thought fit to return? Cease complaining then, and prepare to quit this place for Rome at a moment's notice." On hearing this, young Tullius, with his usual rashness, replied in haste (*Orat. Rect.*), "I have no more to say; but I should like to inform you that your warnings, whether they are wise or unwise, have not the slightest effect upon me: and I shall judge for myself, without the interference of others, whether it is better

to go to Rome or to remain at Carthage. I never asked anyone to spare me or to pity me, and I ask no one now."

64. When the general had heard this, he turned with fury to his brave officers, Tullius and Balbus, and said (*Orat. Obl.*), "Why did you not tell me of this before I came here? Now that it is too late to help our countrymen, you come with the sad news that almost the whole of our army is destroyed, that 1,400 of the infantry have been slain, that the cavalry have fled to their respective homes, and there is no hope left. What was there to prevent you from bridging over the river and marching upon Rome. If even a single regiment out of your vast army had done this, you would have penetrated without resistance into the heart of the enemy's country." Hearing this, the officers threw themselves at their general's feet with tears and supplications, and said that they would never desert him, that nothing should induce them to break their faith with him, and that they would spare no one, and pity no one, who dared to accuse him of the slightest fault. All they wanted was, that he would give them a chance of redeeming their character and proving their penitence.

65. After the occupation of the bridge over the river, near the village of Alino, some seventeen miles from their camp, the little band of heroes did not enjoy a long respite from the attacks of the superior force by which they were now completely surrounded. Admirable was the spirit in which they prepared to resist the assault. Although they knew not where to look for succour, and could scarcely hope to succeed if unassisted, they felt that they could do their country good service, even if they only checked the invaders' progress for a few hours; and for such an object as this it seemed to these brave men worth while to risk their lives. In this dangerous position the general made his arrangements with coolness and sagacity. He sent out a few of the swiftest of his cavalry with orders to scour the country for ten miles round, and to bring back word the same day of the position and numbers of the enemy, and whether the attacking force consisted mostly of cavalry or infantry; they were also, if possible, to take a prisoner or two, so as to enable them to gain information of the enemy's plans. The rest of the army was employed, without excepting even the officers, in fortifying all the weakest points of the position. After (*postquam*) all preparations had been completed, the aged general collected his men (and)

addressed them in his usual cheerful way (*Orat. Obl.*):—" I have done," he said, "what I could: the rest depends on you; and I am sure you will not, as the enemy have repeatedly done, promise without performing. I now dismiss you to your several posts, in perfect confidence that you will not live to be pitied, and that none of you will prefer disgrace to death."

66. "The flower that blooms to-day to-morrow dies," says the melodious poet Shelley in one of his sweetest poems; and in truth, poets, moralists, novelists, and philosophers repeat, almost without ceasing, meditations on the transitory nature of every thing in the world, and are never tired of asserting that life is nothing but a dream. It is curious, however, to note the little success that these remarks, in their usual exaggerated form, have had in influencing the actions of practical men. The instinct of the majority of mankind refuses to believe those who would maintain that life is a dream, heroism a delusion, and that there is nothing worth living for. On the contrary, men have felt that there is no position in life but can be made real and noble by acts of self-sacrifice, whether for the benefit of one's country or for that of individuals. I am therefore inclined to prefer to the usual exaggerations of philosophers, the following simple advice which I once heard a father give to his son (*Orat. Obl.*):—" Do not forget the importance that attaches to every action of life. It matters not whether it be great or small; for whether great or small, it can be rightly or wrongly done. That was what the Stoics meant when they said that, even if a bad man merely extended his finger, he sinned; by which they meant that the most trifling action of a bad man must be bad."

67. Ten years after the reduction of this vast kingdom, the Casmathians, led by the intrepid Balbus, made a daring inroad beyond the river Eborius and advanced to Turium, a town some thirty miles off, with no more than 500 horse. By order of Tullius, the king of Turium, the bridge had been broken down to cut off the retreat of Balbus, and the person or head of the rebel was every moment expected. The king's legate, from a motive of fear or pity, having sent a messenger to apprise Balbus of his danger, recommended him to escape with speed. "Although," replied the intrepid Casmathian to the messenger, "your master is at the head of 30,000 men, yet, since he wishes to know what sort of men crossed the Eborius with me, I will shew him that he has not, in all that host, three such men as

these." Then turning to three of his followers, he ordered the first to plunge a dagger into his heart, the second to leap into the Eborius, and the third to cast himself down a precipice. All of them obeyed without uttering a word of remonstrance. "Relate what you have seen," continued Balbus. "Before evening it will be your general, not I, that will need pity. Why do you loiter? Depart, unless you wish to perish; and tell him that twelve hours hence he will be chained among my dogs." Before the evening the camp was surprised, and the threat executed.

68. The haughty Solyman, Emperor of Turkey, in his attack on Hungary, took the city of Belgrade, which was considered with justice the bulwark of Christendom. After this important conquest, a woman of low rank approached him and complained wtih bitterness that some of his soldiers had carried off her cattle one night while she was asleep, and had thus deprived her of her only means of subsistence. "Tell me," said Solyman, with a smile, "how you contrived to sleep so soundly that the robbers did not wake you. I could not have slept so soundly." "True, my sovereign," replied the woman, "I did sleep soundly, but it was in the fullest confidence that your highness watched for the safe y of your poorest subjects."

The magnanimous emperor, instead of resenting this freedom, praised the courage with which she had spoken, and made the poor woman ample amends for the loss she had sustained.

LATIN GENDERS.

First Declension.
Feminine.

Second Declension.
Masculine Endings, er, ir, *and* us.   *Neuter Ending*, um

Exceptions {alvus, colus (m), domus, humus, vannus;
Greek *nouns in* odus, *as* exodus, &c., *with* dialectus, diphthongus, &c.
pelagus, virus, vulgus (m).}

Third Declension.

Masculine Endings.	*Feminine Endings.*	*Neuter Endings.*
er, or, os	do, go, io, as, is, aus, x	C, A, T, E, L, N,
os, *imparisyllabic*	es, *parisyllabic* ; s, *impure*	AR, UR, US *short*,
o, *when not* do, go, io	us, *long, in hypermonosyllables*	US *long, in monosyllables*

Principal Exceptions.

		do cardo ordo udo		
Principal Exceptions.		go harpago ligo margo		*Principal Excepts.*
er CADAVER	ITER	*io nouns not abstract*, as papilio, &c.;		*l* sal sol
PAPAVER	TUBER	also ternio, &c.		
UBER	VER	*as* as elephas vas (*vadis*)		*n* lien pecten
VERBER	linter	VAS (*vasis*) FAS NEFAS		ren splen
or arbor	ÆQUOR	*is* amnis anguis (f) axis cassis (is)		*ur* fur furfur
COR	MARMOR	cinis collis crinis ensis		turtur vultur
		fascis finis (f) follis funis		
os cos	dos	ignis lapis mensis orbis		*us short*, lepus
CHAOS	EPOS	panis piscis postis pulvis		pecus (*udis*)
OS (*oris*)	OS (*ossis*)	sanguis torris unguis vectis		
		vermis		
es compes	merces	*x* calix codex cortex frutex		*us long,* grus (m)
merges	quies	grex pollex silex thorax		sus (m) mus
requies	seges	vertex		
teges	ÆS	*es* acinaces		
		s bidens(f) dens fons hydrops		
o caro	echo	mons pons rudens (f)		

Fourth Declension.
Masculine, *except* acus, idus (pl)., manus, porticus, tribus.

Fifth Declension.
Feminine, *except* dies (f. Poets.), meridies.

A. **Masculine** *by meaning.* Names of Male persons, the Occupations of men, and Winds, Rivers, and Months.

B. **Feminine** „ „ of Females, Countries, Islands, Towns, Plants, and Trees.

Masculine.................Exceptions to B..................Neuter.

Towns. *Some in* O, *as*, Croto, Hippo, &c.	Towns. *All in* um, *or plural* A.
All Plurals in i, *as* Veii, Delphi, &c.	*Those in* E *or* UR *of the third*.
Plants *Those in* er (*and many in* us) *of the second.*	Plants. *Those in* ER *or* UR *of the third*.

SCHEME OF LATIN PRONUNCIATION.*

Based on the nearest English Approximations.

VOWELS AND DIPHTHONGS.

Latin	ā	=	English	*a* in f*a*ther.
,,	ă	=	,,	*first a* in *a*way, or *a* in vill*a*.
,,	ē	=	,,	*ai* in p*ai*n.
,,	ae	=	,,	*ai* in p*ai*n.
,,	oe	=	,,	*ai* in p*ai*n.
,,	ĕ	=	,,	*e* in m*e*n.
,,	ī	=	,,	*i* in mach*i*ne.
,,	ĭ	=	,,	*i* in p*i*ty.
,,	ō	=	,,	*o* in h*o*me.
,,	ŏ	=	,,	*o* in t*o*p.
,,	u	=	,,	*u* in r*u*le.
,,	ŭ	=	,,	*u* in f*u*ll.
,,	au	=	,,	*ow* in p*ow*er.
,,	eu	=	,,	Latin ĕ followed quickly by Latin ŭ (differs little from present pronunciation).
,,	ei	=	,,	Latin ĕ followed quickly by Latin ĭ (differs little from *ai* in p*ai*n).

CONSONANTS.

Latin c, ch	=	English *k*.
,, g	=	,, *g* in *g*et.
,, s	=	,, *s* in *s*in.
,, t (ratio)	=	,, *t* in ca*t*, not *sh*, as in na*t*ion.
,, j	=	,, *y* in *y*ard.
,, v	=	,, *v*.
,, z, ph, th	=	,, *z*, *ph*, *th*.

bs, bt should be sounded and generally written *ps, pt*.
Latin **s** between two vowels = (sometimes) English *s* in ro*s*e, *e.g.* 'ro**s**a.

---

* Taken from the *Syllabus of Latin Pronunciation*, issued by the Professors of Latin at the Universities of Cambridge and Oxford, at the request of the Head Masters of Schools. Some modifications have been made by the suppression of all Italian standards, and of all the English standards of pronunciation that contain a vowel followed by *r*. Consequently the Latin **o** is represented by the English *o*. The Professors give the option of pronouncing **v** as *v* or as *w*.

APPENDIX

ON THE CONNECTION OF SENTENCES.

You may know the Latin equivalents of every word and idiom in the English language, and yet may be unable to write Latin Prose. For to write Prose you must also know how to connect together the different parts of a Latin sentence, and the different sentences of a Latin passage. For this purpose the following rules may be useful. They rise naturally out of the colloquial nature of English as contrasted with the logical nature of Latin:

I. English prefers co-ordinate, Latin subordinate clauses.

II. English prefers multiplicity of subjects, Latin one subject.

III. English omits connecting particles, Latin inserts them.

IV. English uses epithets, Latin uses subordinate clauses.

I. *He took and burned the bridge* — Pontem **captum** incendit

II. *They asked him his opinion, and he replied, &c.* — **Rogatus** (or **interrogantibus**) sententiam respondit

III. When you have a group of abrupt English sentences connected perhaps by no Conjunctions at all, or by *and* (which may mean anything)—*e.g.* (1) '*The king refused the petition*; (2) *The queen was delighted*'—you must ask, first, which is the most important sentence in the group? secondly, what is the relation between this, the most important sentence, and others that are less important? The most important sentence must be as it were the spine, of the sentence, and the less important must be the vertebræ, and must be carefully connected with the spine. A Latin period is vertebrate.

But how are we to connect each of the vertebræ with the spine? What is to be our connecting particle in each case? The English will not help us much here: for the connecting particles in English are like the vowel points in Hebrew—they are not written, but must be deduced from the context, and must be expressed by the voice. For example, above, the relation of sentence (2) to sentence (1) is that of (*a*) *consequence* to *cause*, and this may be expressed in two ways, either by a *forward link*: '*Quod* **quum** rex negavisset se facturum, regina præ gaudio exultabat,' or by a backward link, '**Quod** or **quæ res** reginam summo gaudio affecit' or, '*Regina* **igitur**,' or, '**Itaque** regina.' But alter (2) above, and you must alter your connecting particle.

APPENDIX.

Thus, for 'the queen *was delighted*' write

'The queen
- (*b*) was still patient' (*contrariety*).
- (*c*) had not shown her usual tact' (*cause* of the king's refusal).
- (*d*) left the room in anger' (*immediate sequence*).
- (*e*) insulted the petitioners' (*simultaneousness*, or *addition*).
- (*f*) saw that all was lost (*consequence late but inevitable*, **tum vero**, or, **tum demum**).
- (*g*) had anticipated this' (*precedence*, **jam antea**).

All these different sentences will require different *forward* or *backward links:* some of these are:—

FORWARD LINKS: **quum, quia, quoniam, quamvis, ut** (although), **quanquam, ita (ut), tam—quam, antequam, priusquam, donec, simul ac, dum, partim, non solum, quum (...tum), simul (...simul), aut** (either), **et** (*both*). **si, nisi, &c.**

The Participle is also used as a forward link, **rogatus**, *when he was asked*; and so are **ut** and **qui** in the phrases **cujus erat stultitiæ, ut erat semper stultus**.

BACKWARD LINKS: **Nam, enim, quippe, itaque, igitur, idcirco, quocirca, quamobrem, quare, autem, vero, verum, sed, at, quanquam** (*and yet*), **jam, interim, interea, confestim, mox, deinde, postremo, denique, tum demum, porro, præterea, huc accedebat ut**. Above all. the Relative Pronoun is thus used, *e.g.* '**quæ** quum ita sint,' '**quibus** auditis,' '**quod** quum intellexisset,' and '**quod** si,' which last is almost equivalent to our '*and* if.' It will be a useful exercise to classify these *links* or conjunctions according to their meaning.

Sometimes a backward link is rendered unnecessary by an emphatic word at the beginning of the sentence, referring to the previous sentence, *e.g.* 'Nec vero ulla vis imperii tanta est ut premente metu possit esse diuturna. **Testis** est Phalaris, &c.' So especially **idem** for 'he also.' See Par. 46.

IV. Under the head of Omission of Connecting Particles comes the English use of *implied statement* or *innuendo*; e.g. 'The *haughty* monarch refused to listen to the remonstrances of his ministers.' Here the *epithet* 'haughty' implies the *reason* why the monarch did not listen. The conversational English, disliking subordinate sentences, prefers to *imply* the reason in an epithet: the logical Latin prefers to *express* it: '**cujus** erat semper superbiæ,' '**ut** erat natura superbus.'

ALPHABETICAL INDEX.

The references (unless the page is specially mentioned) are to the PARAGRAPHS.

	Par.
A	22
Ablative, meaning of	28*
,, in **i** and **e**.	Page 115*
,, when used	28-32
,, after Deponents	13
Abstract Nouns not frequent in Latin	3*a*
Accusative, before and after Infinitive, ambiguous	48
Adjectives, not doubled	12
Adverbs, Adverbial Phrases	24, 25
After, Conjunction	11
Alius	7
All, '*all that*,' &c.	54
Also, in 'he *also*' = **idem**	46
Alter	7
And he = **qui**	46
And omitted	47
And '*and* no one, *nothing*, &c.'	45
Another	7
Antequam, when followed by Subjunctive	66
Any	7
Apodosis, meaning of	69*
As ... as	59
As long as	11
Ask, '*I ask to*'	Page 89
At, '*at* enim'	44*a*
Attribute, the	18
Autem, different from **sed**	44*a*
Auxiliary Verbs	12
Because, 'not *because* ... but *because*'	68
Before, Conjunction	11
But omitted	47
But, when **sed**, when **autem**	44*a*
But, 'there's no one *but*'	55
Celo, construction of	14
Come, '*I come* to see'	72
Command, '*I command* him to'	Page 89
Command in oratio obliqua	78*c*
Comparative of Adjectives in -**eus**, -**ius**, -**uus**	Page 21†
Comparison, expressed by **quam**	61
Comparison, expressed by the Ablative	62
Conditional Sentences	69
Conjunctions	43-72
,, Coordinate	44

	Par.
Conjunctions, Coordinate and Subordinate	43
Conjunctions, of Condition	69
,, of Purpose	72
,, of Reason	67
,, Negative	45
,, Enclitic	44*a*
,, Subordinate	48
Connection of Sentences	Page 164
Could	Page 10
Cum, mecum, &c.	Page 56
Dative after Verbs and Adjectives	6, 13
Dative after Verbs of Motion	15
Dative of Design (Double Dative)	17
Debui	13
Dependent Interrogative	53
Dignus followed by Abl.	32
Domum	16
Dum followed by Pres. Tense	11
Each	7
Ellipse of Prepositions	42
,, of Verb after Conjunctions	70
Emptiness, expressed by Abl.	31
Enclitics	44*a*
Epithet, implying cause	Page 6
Et omitted	44
Et non, to be avoided	45
Ex, '**ex** itinere'	39
Extension, expressed by Acc.	27
Every	22
Fear, I (construction)	49
Fertur	49
First, 'he was the *first to*'	Page 91
Fit, 'he is not *fit to* &c.'	Page 90
For, '*for* ten minutes'	27
Fulness, expressed by Abl.	30
Future Participle, how expressed in Inceptives.	Page 98
Genitive after **accuso, absolvo**	36
Genitive after Impers. Verbs	13*a*
,, ,, Participial Adj.	34
,, ,, other Adj.	35
,, of Quality	37
,, Objective	33
,, after Adjectives and Participles	34, 5

INDEX.

	Par.
Genitive after Verbs of Accusing, &c.	36
Gerund, after what Prepositions	75
Gerundive	75
,, used impersonally	5
Great, 'this *great* calamity'	19
Having, '*having* said' (end)	66
Him = to him	13
Him = **se**	10*a*, 78*f*
Hope, 'I hope *to*, *that*'	Page 88
Idem, = he also	46
If, '*if* he comes'	11
,, 'he asked *if*'	51
,, '*if* so,' '*if* not'	70
Igitur, where placed	44*a*
Impersonal Verbs	13*a*
In, '*in* anger'	24
Indignus, followed by Abl.	32
Infinitive Future	Page 98
,, and **Acc** ambig.	48
Instead of	Page 95
Interest	13*a*
Interrogative, Dependent	53
,, in Orat. Obliqua	78*d*
Islands, case of, after verbs of motion	16
It, '*it* was John *that* &c.'	4
,, redundant	5
,, '*it* is said that'	5
Ita followed by **si**	Page 85
,, meaning of	71
Jam, different from **nunc**.	25
Jubeo, Construction of	Page 89
Like, 'a man *like* Cato'	60
Locative Case	1
Magis, different from **plus**	25
Magni	29
Mea interest	13*a*
Measure of excess	42
Metaphors	79
Minoris	29
Modo = *only*	25
More, '*more* than a hundred'	63
,, when **magis**, when **plus**	25
Motion, Verbs implying	15
,, Verbs of	16
Multo with Comparative	42
Must	12
Ne in Prohibition	12
Ne for **ut** . . . **non**	72
Nemine, avoid	10
Neminis, avoid	10
Nemo = *no*	22
Neque, not **et non**	45
Neuter, used Adverbially	14

	Par.
No, '*no* poet'	22
Nostri, Genitive, when used.	10
Nostrum, Genitive, when used	10
Not, '*not* because'	68
Now, **jam, nunc**	25
,, Conj. turned by **Rel.**	46
Nullius, not **neminis**	10
Nullo, not **nemine**	10
Nunc, different from **jam**	25
Object, Indirect	14
Objective Genitive	33
Of after Participles	34
Of = *made of*	37
,, redundant	40
One	8, 9
Once, when **semel**, when **forte**, when **quondam**	25
Only	25
Oratio Obliqua	78*a*
,, **Recta**	78
Other, 'the *other*'	7
Ought	Page 10
Parentheses	77
Participle Present (English)	23, 74
Parvi	29
Passive English rendered impersonally	6
Passive English ambiguous	11
Paullo with Comparatives	42
Personifications, not so frequent in Latin as in English	79
Persuaded, I am	6
Pluris	29
Plus, different from **magis**	25
Point of time	28
Postquam	11, 66
Potui	12
Prepositions, Alphabetical Dictionary of	41
Prepositions, between two Nouns	33
Prepositions, Ellipse of	42
,, local meanings of	26
Prepositions implying Rest or Motion	39
Prepositions, Verbs compounded with	15
Prepositional phrases	20
Price	29
Prius-quam, when followed by Subjunctive	66
Prohibition	12
Promise, 'I *promise* to'	Page 88
Pronouns	7–10
,, how avoided	76

INDEX.

	Par.
Protasis, meaning of	69*
Provided that	Page 83
Quam	61
Quamvis	Page 84
Quanquam	,, 84
Quanti	29
Question, Dependent	53
,, in Oratio Obliqua	78d
Qui	52
Quidam = *a*	22
Quidem to be separated from ne	45
Quidquid hominum	20
Quilibet, quivis, when used	7
Quin followed by **futurum sit**	49
Quisquam, nec quisquam	45
,, when used 7, Page 113†
Quisque	7
,, used after a Superlative Adjective	22
Quivis	7
Quum	66
Refert	13a
Reflexive Verbs	13a
Relative Pronoun	52-59
,, omitted	58
Relative precedes Antecedent	54
Relatival Conjunctions	59
Rus	16
Se, distinguished from **illum**.	10a
Sed ,, **autem**	44a
Sequence of Tenses	64
Should	12
Si	69
Sive and **utrum**	Page 85
Solum — '*only*'	25
Subjunctive, after Relative Pronoun	52
Subjunctive, when used after Conjunctions of Time	66
Sum, with Double Dative	17
Supine, 'venio **visum**'	75
Supposing	Page 83
Suus, ipsius	Page 102
Tanti	29
Tantum = '*only*'	25
Tenses	11
Tenses, sequence of	64
Than	61-63
That, Conjunction	48, 49
,, '*that . . . not*' = **ne**	72
,, 'there's no doubt *that*'	49
,, 'I fear *that*'	49
,, 'it is said *that*'	49
,, 'it seems *that*'	49
That, Pronoun	5

	Par
That, distinguished from *who*	52
,, '*the* most beautiful *that*'	54
,, after repeated Antecedent	56
,, for *when*	57
,, '*that . . . not*' = **quin**	55
The, uses of	21
The, '*the* battle of Cannæ'	20
,, '*the* men in the ship'	20
,, '*the* river Tiber'	18
,, '*the* timid dove'	18
This, '*this* great calamity'	19
Though	Page 84
Till, Conjunction	11
Time, extension of	27
Time, point of	28
To, different meanings of	73
Too, '*too—to*'	Page 90
Towns, after Verbs of Motion	16
Tum demum	Page 85
Ullus	7
Unless	Par. 11, Page 85
Uterque	7
Utinam	72
Utrum, used in Dependent Interrogatives	51
Verbal, after Prepositions	75
,, English use of	75
Verbs, Auxiliary	12
,, followed by *to*	73
,, ,, *that*	49
Verbs, compounded with Prepositions	15
,, followed by the Abl.	13
,, ,, two Acc.	14
,, ,, Dat. 6 13, 15
,, ,, Genitive	13
,, ,, **ut** Page 89
,, Impersonal	13a
Vereor (construction)	49
Vero different from **verum**	44
Verum different from **vero**	44
Vestri, Genitive, when used	10
Vestrum, Genitive, when used	7
Videtur	49
What, double use of	53
When, '*when* he comes'	11
Whether, when **utrum**, when **sive**	51
While, followed by Eng. Past, Lat. Pres.	11
While, (logical) omitted	47
,, not temporal	87
,, '*while* walking'	70
Who, different from *that*	52
With, '*with* anger'	24
Without, *With* Verbal	Page 96
Would	12

www.ingramcontent.com/pod-product-compliance
Lightning Source LLC
Chambersburg PA
CBHW021729220426
43662CB00008B/764